Teachings
from the
Mani Retreat

MAY THE BUDDHADHARMA REACH ALL SENTIENT BEINGS · LAMA YESHE WISDOM ARCHIVE ·

Previously published by the

LAMA YESHE WISDOM ARCHIVE

Becoming Your Own Therapist, by Lama Yeshe

Advice for Monks and Nuns, by Lama Yeshe and Lama Zopa Rinpoche

Virtue and Reality, by Lama Zopa Rinpoche

Make Your Mind an Ocean, by Lama Yeshe

Teachings from the Vajrasattva Retreat, by Lama Zopa Rinpoche

Daily Purification: A Short Vajrasattva Practice, by Lama Zopa Rinpoche

The Essence of Tibetan Buddhism, by Lama Yeshe

Making Life Meaningful, by Lama Zopa Rinpoche

FOR INITIATES ONLY

A Chat about Heruka, by Lama Zopa Rinpoche

A Chat about Yamantaka, by Lama Zopa Rinpoche

May whoever sees, touches, reads, remembers, or talks or thinks about these booklets never be reborn in unfortunate circumstances, receive only rebirths in situations conducive to the perfect practice of Dharma, meet only perfectly qualified spiritual guides, quickly develop bodhicitta and immediately attain enlightenment for the sake of all sentient beings.

TEACHINGS
from the
MANI RETREAT

Chenrezig Institute, December 2000

LAMA ZOPA RINPOCHE

Edited by
Ailsa Cameron

LAMA YESHE WISDOM ARCHIVE
Boston

www.LamaYeshe.com
A non-profit charitable organization for the benefit of
all sentient beings and a section of the
Foundation for the Preservation of the Mahayana Tradition
www.fpmt.org

First published 2001

10,000 copies for free distribution

Please contact the LAMA YESHE WISDOM ARCHIVE for copies of our free books

Lama Yeshe Wisdom Archive
PO Box 356, Weston, MA 02493 USA

ISBN 1-891868-10-1
10 9 8 7 6 5 4 3 2 1

Cover photograph by Nick Dawson

Book design by L.J.Sawlit

Printed in Canada on recycled, acid-free paper

CONTENTS

Publisher's Acknowledgments

WE ARE EXTREMELY GRATEFUL to our friends and supporters who have made it possible for the LAMA YESHE WISDOM ARCHIVE to both exist and function: to Lama Yeshe and Lama Zopa Rinpoche, whose kindness is impossible to repay; to Peter and Nicole Kedge and Venerable Ailsa Cameron for helping bring the ARCHIVE to its present state of development; to Venerable Roger Kunsang, Lama Zopa's tireless assistant, for his kindness and consideration; and to our sustaining supporters: Drs. Penny Noyce & Leo Liu, Barry & Connie Hershey, Joan Terry, Roger & Claire Ash-Wheeler, Claire Atkins, Ecie Hursthouse, Lily Chang Wu, T. Y. Alexander, Therese Miller, Chris Dornan, Henry & Catherine Lau, Tom & Suzanne Castles, Datuk Tai Tsu Kuang, Chuah Kok Leng, the Caytons (Lori, Karuna, Pam, Bob & Amy), Tom Thorning, Tan Swee Eng, Salim Lee, Doren & Mary Harper, Claire Ritter, Sandra Magnussen, Cecily Drucker, Lynnea Elkind, Janet Moore, Su Hung, Carol Davies, Jack Morison, Dorian Ribush and Dharmawati Brechbuhl. We also thank most sincerely Massimo Corona and the FPMT International Office for their generous financial and administrative assistance.

We would also like to acknowledge the great kindness of Richard Gere and the Gere Foundation for so compassionately supporting the ARCHIVE since its inception and for making a generous grant to help cover the printing of this book, and to thank Jennifer Greenfield for her kind assistance over these many years.

We are especially indebted to our kind friends in Australia who specifically contributed to this book: Ven. Ailsa Cameron, Alan Carter, Chenrezig Nuns' Community, Ven. Losang Chodron, Ven. Chonyi,

Colin Crosbie, Caroline Crossman, Ven. Dechen, Ven. Thubten Drolkar, Ven. Losang Drolkar, Dung Lam Family, The Enlightenment Project, Krissie Foulkes, Mark and Dechen Gerrard, Helena, Su Hung, Ven. Tenzin Jangchub, Ven. Jinpa, Roger Johnson, Ven. Yeshe Khadro, Gayle Laverty, Ven. Carolyn Lawler, Tammy Le, Ven. Jampa Legdan, Ven. Losang Lhagsam, Mani Retreat Fund, Alan Marsh, Ven. Margaret McAndrew, Carolyn McLeod, Kara McLeod, Priscilla McNamara, Ven. Namdag, Peter Nelson, Jo Newman, Justine Newport, Lan Nguyen, Annette Norris, Pam, Eddie Peet, Julie Pham, Helen Pryor, Nicholas Redmond, Samantabhadra Offering Circle, Debbie Smith, Sandy Smith, Ken Somers, Ven. Tardö, Ven. Tsapel, Vecchi Family, Kathy Vichta, Hadden Williamson, Ven. Yangdzom

We would like, as well, to express our appreciation for the kindness and compassion of all those generous benefactors who have contributed to the ARCHIVE since our last publication, *The Essence of Tibetan Buddhism*. Therefore, for donations received between February and May, 2001, we extend a huge thank you to Judy B. Adams, Ven. Bob Alcorn, Jan Victoria Angel, Leticia Anson, Rako Araki, Christine Arlington, Yong Meng Beh, Peggy Bennington, Allan Bomhard, Avi Bonfil, Donald Bonney, Melanie Bryan, Buddha Maitreya Study Group, Candy Campbell, Sharon Cardamone, John Carmody, Kendra Carpenter, Chang Jin Meng & Family, Chew Min Chuan, Michael Childs, Larry Chiriboga, Neil Christopherson, Chung Kim Chuan, Maggie Claydon, John Edward Custy III, MaryAnn Czermak, Jonathan Danziger, Nan Deal, John Deluca, Jhamba Dolkar, Richard Donnelly, Herbert J. Dorris, Jan Eldridge, Sarah Feifel, Ven. Damchö Finnegan, Dionne Fomby, Sesame Fowler, Krishna Kanta Ghosh, Sha Anna Gleason, Ken Goddard, Stanley Goldberg, Carleen Gonder, Bob Gottlieb, Alnis Grants & Aryatara Institute, Holly June Graves, Laura Guerreiro-Ramos, James Hagan,

Judith A. Hardenburg, Richard Hay, Lella Heins, Silke Heleine, Myron Helmer, Bosco Ho, Wendy Hobbs, Larry Howe, Sandra Howell, T.Y. Hsieh, Elaine Jackson, John Jackson, Roger Jackson, James W. Johns, Gay Judson, Bill Kelley & Robyn Brentano, Toni Kenyon, Allan W. King, Camille Kozlowski, Dieter Kratzer, Jasmine Krotkov, Lorne & Terry Ladner, Chiu-Mei Lai & Anthony Stowe, Willem Langelaan, Melanie Law, Harry Leong, John Liberty, Loh Seng, Ky Truong Ly, Janusz Madej, Ingrid J. Magdahl, Len Martin Jr., Fred Martinson, Phil McDonald, Robert McDonough, Ellen McInerny, S. McKelvey, Hope McLeod, John McMann, Sybil Miller, Radmila Moacanin, Kalleen Mortensen, Carol Moss, Ven. Thubten Munsel, Robert Mueller, Michael Myers, Wanda Nettl, John & Beth Newman, Giang Nguyen, Kimchung Nguyen, Emi Okuda, Janet Olsen, Jeri Opalk, Gregory & Anna Osborne, Chris Overall, Pek See Ah Peng, James Pelkey, Robert Phipps, Michele Picozzi Paterson, Giovanna Pescetti, George Propps, Karen Rice, Wendy Ridley, Rev. Janyce Riedel, P. Rind, Tamara Salmutter, Jesse Sartain, Angie Sassano, K.B. Schaetzel-Hill, Douglas Schamerhorn, Alexandria Schiller, James Schmitt, Amy Sedivy, Ajna Seret, Rebecca Seslar, Deanna Sheriff, Beth Lee Simon, E. Gene Smith, Ed Softky, Khuslen Soninbayar, Jack Sonnabaum & Judith Hunt, Robert Soto, Sheridan Sperry, Gareth Sparham, Margaret Spoor, Jennifer Sprowl, Lana Sundberg, Vincenzo Tallarico, Janet Tan, Sandra Tatlock, Thubten Norbu Ling, Sandra & Sander Tiderman, Wilhelmina van de Poll, Lerie Alstad von Ells, Robbie Watkins, Susan Webster, Jane Werner & Lobsang Aye Rinpoche, Kate Lila Wheeler, Joseph Williams, Jan Willis, Carol Arredondo Wolovsky and Murray Wright.

Great thanks are also due to the following Australian supporters who contributed through our Melbourne office and have not been specifically thanked before: Will & Lyndy Abram, Roger Amos, Atisha

Centre, Nella Binnendijk, Norma Brahatis, Buddhist Library Meditation Centre, Ven. Losang Chodron, Gerda Cohen, Christine Conlon, Ven. Thubten Dolma, Brian Dwyer, Frances Kelly, Langri Tangpa Centre, Yvonne Malykke, Shirley Marshall, Carolyn McLeod, Pauline McLoughlin, Debby Mientjes, Nancy Patton, David Roberts, Zarna & Anil Somaia, Ken Somers, Adam Struzynski, Vajrasattva Mountain Centre, Diana van Die, Theo van Embden and Ingrid Vickery-Howe.

We would also like to thank the many kind people who have asked that their donations be kept anonymous; the volunteers who have given so generously of their time to help us with our mailings; Alison Ribush & Mandala Books (Melbourne) for much appreciated assistance with our work in Australia; and Dennis Heslop, Philip Bradley and our other friends at Wisdom Books (London) for their great help with our work in Europe.

Finally, we are most grateful to Ven. Ailsa Cameron for her skillful editing of these and many other of Lama Zopa Rinpoche's teachings over the years, to Nick Dawson for so kindly offering us the cover photograph and to L.J. Sawlit for donating her time to design this beautiful book.

If you, dear reader, would like to join this noble group of open-hearted altruists by contributing to the production of more free booklets by Lama Yeshe or Lama Zopa Rinpoche or to any other aspect of the LAMA YESHE WISDOM ARCHIVE's work, please contact us to find out how.

—*Dr. Nicholas Ribush*

Through the merit of having contributed to the spread of the Buddha's teachings for the sake of all sentient beings, may our benefactors and their families and friends have long and healthy lives, all happiness, and may all their Dharma wishes be instantly fulfilled.

EDITOR'S PREFACE

THIS BOOK IS AN EDITED TRANSCRIPT of teachings given by Lama Zopa Rinpoche from December 22 to 26, 2000, as part of the inaugural Mani Retreat at Chenrezig Institute in Queensland, Australia.

Rinpoche first mentioned the idea of organizing a retreat at Chenrezig Institute to recite one hundred million OM MANI PADME HUMs in March 1999 during the Vajrasattva retreat at Land of Medicine Buddha in California. After mentioning that he would like to organize such retreats in ten different countries, Rinpoche went on to say, "I thought one retreat could happen at Chenrezig Institute in Australia, but I am not sure. It might be difficult. People could recite the mantras individually, but it might not be so easy for them to recite the mantras in a group for a long time."

When Rinpoche visited Chenrezig Institute in April 2000, however, it became obvious that, difficult or not, such a retreat was to be organized. After introducing the idea of having a Chenrezig Celebration each year in which extensive offerings would be made to the large Chenrezig thangka currently being painted by Peter Iseli, Rinpoche said, "I would like Chenrezig Institute to organize every year the reciting of one hundred million OM MANI PADME HUMs. There are many FPMT centers here in Australia, but since this center has the name 'Chenrezig Institute,' I would like the hundred million manis to be organized here."

Because of the busy study program at Chenrezig Institute, it was decided that the retreat could only be held over the summer break—not a very appealing prospect as Queensland summers are hot, humid and filled with biting insects. With this in mind, the gompa was screened and new ceiling fans installed. The task of actually reciting one hundred million OM MANI PADME HUMs seemed impossible. Even if the retreat ran for one hundred days, one million mantras would need to be recited every single day. In any case, it was decided to begin the retreat on November 26, 2000, and end it on the morning of *lo-sar* (Tibetan new year's day), February 24, 2001.

Prior to the start of the retreat, Rinpoche sent further advice on the actual structure of the retreat and an invitation to join the retreat (see Prologue). Rinpoche suggested that the Eight Mahayana Precepts be taken each morning, that the first session be the *Combined Jorchö and Lama Chöpa Puja*, and that the mani sessions be based on the *Nyung-nä Sadhana*, with prostrations to the Thirty-five Buddhas and recitation of a *lam-rim* prayer as preliminaries. Extensive dedication prayers were also to be made at the end of the final session of the day. In addition, Rinpoche suggested that one thousand water bowls be offered each day (or at least a minimum of twenty sets of offerings).

Once the retreat started it quickly became apparent that we couldn't hope to recite one million manis each day. By the time Rinpoche arrived for his eagerly anticipated visit late on December 20, we had recited a total of just four million mantras. After a rest day, Rinpoche began attending many of the retreat sessions. Initially he observed closely what was happening and scribbled down notes about suggested improvements. Over the subsequent days he fine-tuned the retreat, shortening the time spent on prostrations (to everyone's relief!), adding prayers and motivations and suggesting different tunes for some of the chants. The practice became richer and deeper. Because many new people with no prior knowledge of Buddhism joined in the retreat, Rinpoche also took time to introduce them to some of the practices involved.

In the final session that Rinpoche attended, he mentioned how much he had enjoyed participating in the retreat: "I enjoyed the sessions I attended here *very* much. I think this practice is really fantastic. It is something that you find more and more inspiring—not something that becomes more and more boring. The more sessions you do, the more inspiring it becomes." While sad that Rinpoche could join us for only a short period, we continued the retreat with fresh inspiration and insight. Before he left, Rinpoche extended the period of mantra recitation to Saka Dawa, June 6, 2001, and also gave permission for manis to be recited at home.

By the end of the retreat in the gompa, just over twenty-five million manis had been recited. More than ninety people attended the final session of the retreat and then enjoyed a sumptuous breakfast in the Lama Yeshe Big Love Café.

I would like to thank Rinpoche for his infinite kindness and compassion, and especially for participating in the Mani Retreat and giving the inspiring teachings contained in this book. I would also like to thank Chenrezig Institute for hosting the retreat; the organizing committee for planning the details of the retreat; the benefactors and sponsors who supported the retreat; Ven. Connie Miller of the FPMT Education Department for her dedicated efforts in preparing the booklets *Combined Jorchö and Lama Chöpa Puja, Lam-Rim Prayers* and *Dedication Prayers* for use during the retreat; all the nuns of the Chenrezig Nuns' Community for sustaining the retreat and offering thousands of water bowls, but especially Vens. Margaret McAndrew, Tenzin Tsapel, Tenzin Namdag, Tenzin Chodron, Thubten Jinpa and Thubten Dechen for their skill and dedication in helping lead the retreat sessions; and everyone who participated in the retreat.

May all the merit from the Mani Retreat and the publication of this book be dedicated as directed by Rinpoche in a letter to His Holiness the Dalai Lama:

The Mani Retreat is dedicated to the long life of Your Holiness and for Your Holiness's wishes to succeed immediately, particularly Your Holiness's wish for the Tibetan people to get their country back and to have total freedom. Also, for the officials in mainland China to transform their minds, to totally devote themselves to Your Holiness, to do exactly what Your Holiness wishes and to invite Your Holiness to China to give teachings to millions of people, so that there is the happiness of Dharma, like the sun rising, in the lives of many millions of Chinese people. The retreat is also dedicated to world peace.

Also, may Lama Ösel Rinpoche be able to benefit sentient beings and spread the Dharma like Lama Tsong Khapa, by showing the same qualities as Lama Tsong Khapa.

May all the wishes and projects of Chenrezig Institute be most beneficial for other sentient beings. May we be able to spread the purest teaching of Lama Tsong Khapa in the minds of sentient beings and immediately be able to pacify the sufferings of body and mind of sentient beings. May everyone who comes to Chenrezig Institute be able to have the realization of bodhicitta in this life.

Please guide us, the students of the FPMT, and especially the people who recite the mani mantras, in all our future lifetimes without separation from you, Compassion Buddha.

PROLOGUE

RINPOCHE'S INVITATION TO JOIN THE MANI RETREAT

The benefits of reciting the Compassion Buddha mantra are infinite, like the limitless sky.

Even if you don't have much intellectual understanding of Dharma, even if the only thing you know is OM MANI PADME HUM, still the happiest life is one lived with an attitude free of the eight worldly concerns. If you live your life with that pure attitude free of attachment clinging to this life and spend your life just chanting OM MANI PADME HUM—this six-syllable mantra that is the essence of all Dharma—that's the purest Dharma.

It looks very simple, very easy to recite, but when you think of the benefits, it's not simple at all. Here I'm going to mention just the essence of its infinite benefits.

Reciting this Compassion Buddha mantra once completely purifies the four defeats of breaking the four root vows of self-liberation [*pratimoksha* vows] and the five uninterrupted negative karmas.[1]

It is said in the tantra *Padmatrawa* that it purifies the four root falls and the five uninterrupted negative karmas, and that all other negative karma without exception also gets purified.

It is also said in the discourse called *Exalted Eleven-Faced One*,

Bhagawan (Destroyed, Qualified, Gone Beyond), my heart mantra has such great miracle power that by reciting it just once, the four root downfalls of self-liberation are purified.

If you recite this mantra precisely, as explained in the text, there is no question that you will receive all these benefits.

It is also mentioned in the tantras that you achieve the four qualities of being born in the Amitabha Buddha and other pure lands; at the time of death, seeing Buddha and lights appearing in the sky (meaning white light or different colored clouds); devas making you offerings; and never going to the lower realms [the hell, hungry ghost and animals realms]. You will go to the pure land of Buddha or be reborn as a happy transmigratory being.

It is also written in the tantric text *Padma Chöpen gyi Gyud*:

> Sons and daughters of the race, whoever recites even once the mantra OM MANI PADME HUM while thinking of me or just remembers or keeps [the mantra] on their body purifies the five uninterrupted negative karmas, the five close uninterrupted negative karmas[2] and all other negative karmas and abandons the eight realms where there is no opportunity to practice Dharma: hell, preta, animal realm and so forth.
>
> One will not experience suffering of body, speech and mind. One will be free from fears of vicious animals, cannibals, human beings, non-human beings and sickness. One will actualize the meaning of the Dharmakaya; one will see the holy face of Great Compassion, the Rupakaya.

When one who recites ten malas a day goes swimming, whether in a river, ocean or some other body of water, the water that touches that person's body gets blessed.

It is said that up to seven generations of that person's descendents won't get reborn in the lower realms. The reason for this is that due to the power of mantra, the body is blessed by the person reciting the mantra and visualizing his or her body in form of the holy body of Chenrezig. As a result of such practice, the person's body becomes so powerful, so blessed that it affects the consciousness up to seven generations and also has the effect that even if that person dies with a non-virtuous thought, he or she is not reborn in a lower realm.

Thus, when a person who has recited ten malas of OM MANI PADME HUM a day goes into a river or an ocean, the water that touches the person's body gets blessed, and this blessed water then purifies all the billions and billions of sentient beings in the water. So it's unbelievably beneficial; this person saves the animals in that water from the most unbelievable suffering of the lower realms.

When such a person walks down a road and the wind touches his or her body and then goes on to touch insects, their negative karma gets purified, and it causes them to have a good rebirth. Similarly, when such a person does massage or otherwise touches others' bodies, those people's negative karma also gets purified.

Such a person becomes meaningful to behold; being seen and touched becomes a means of liberating other sentient beings. If a person who has done a *nyung-nä* well is standing on top of a mountain and is seen by someone down below, the negative karma of the person below gets purified.

Some of these benefits are mentioned in the tantra *Thuk-je Chenpo Tön-shak-pe Gyü.*

This means that even the person's breath touching the bodies of other sentient beings purifies their negative karma. Anybody who drinks the water in which such a person has swum gets purified.

Quoting from a tantric text, a very high Amdo lama, Kungthang Jampel Yang, said,

If you are able to request from the heart, if you just do nyung-nä for one day and recite the six-syllable mantra, even though you have created the negative karma to be reborn in the hell realm without break and burn there for years equaling the sand grains of this big earth, those karmas get purified.

Kungthang Jampel Yang also said,

You have collected limitless negative karma during beginningless rebirths and even in this life may have transgressed the three vows, collected negative karma with your gurus, vajra friends and the holy objects of the Three Rare Sublime Ones, and carelessly used polluted food and so forth [food offered by people with devotion or which was offered to the Sangha community by people with faith]. Abiding thus on the precipice of the hell realms, when you meet such Dharma as this, if you have a mind, you have no choice. You must put all your capacity into this practice.

It is also written in the sutra called *Sa-ma-to Go-pe Do*:

If this six-syllable mantra is written by hand on rocks or on stone walls and men, women or children or any other sentient being touch it by hand or simply look at it, through merely seeing it they become bodhisattvas of the end of samsara.

In a text he composed, the very learned Sera-je Geshe, Geshe

Jampa Chodrag, says,

> Thus, by meditating on the holy body of Compassion
> Buddha just once, hearing the holy name just once or
> memorizing it or seeing the six-syllable mantra written
> or just touching it by hand, one gets protected from
> spirits called *de* and spirits called za, which cause para-
> lysis, from yamas, evil vicious animals, diseases, dangers
> and harm from human beings and non-human beings,
> and whatever wishes of this life one has—such as for
> long life, wealth, power and so forth—get fulfilled
> exactly as wished. Then the five uninterrupted negative
> karmas and so forth, such as extremely heavy negative
> karma collected during beginningless time, get purified,
> and one receives good rebirths in all one's future lives.
> And one is able to see Compassion Buddha's holy face
> and so forth.
>
> If it is said that there are such limitless skies of ben-
> efits from remembering the qualities of Arya
> Compassionate-Eyed One and remembering the kind-
> ness and blessings and even just reciting the holy name,
> then one must attempt to practice, making offerings
> and requests and so forth.

These comments come from a text by Geshe Jampa Chodrak, and I
also say the same thing.

We are unbelievably fortunate to have met the Dharma and to
have the opportunity to do recitation and meditation on the
Compassion Buddha. It is an easy way of purifying whatever negative karma we have collected in not only this life but in many previous lives as well.

Because we have met the Buddhadharma, and especially this method—the practice of the Compassion Buddha and recitation of his mantra—it is easy to purify negative karma and collect extensive merit and thus to achieve enlightenment. We are unbelievably fortunate.

Therefore, there is nothing more foolish than not taking advantage of this great opportunity. Normally, we get continuously distracted and waste our lives. Not only that, but all actions done with ego and the three poisonous minds of anger, attachment and ignorance create negative karma, the cause of suffering. In all existence, there is nothing more foolish than using this perfect human body to create only suffering.

In places such as Tibet, Nepal, India and Ladakh, there's a well-established tradition of doing the Compassion Buddha retreat and reciting one hundred million OM MANI PADME HUM mantras. The one held at Chenrezig Institute is the first such retreat in the West and the first in the FPMT organization. This is to happen at Chenrezig once each year—*only* once each year!

If you're feeling guilt in your life, you can overcome it through the purification of attending this retreat.

The retreat is not just chanting mantras with sadhanas, but also includes taking the Eight Mahayana Precepts, if not every day, at least frequently. Whatever merit you collect that day increases 100,000 times. This becomes such a quick and easy way to purify, collect extensive merit, achieve enlightenment and liberate sentient beings from unimaginable suffering and bring them to enlightenment quickly.

Whoever attends a mani retreat is unbelievably fortunate. Even if you can't attend the whole retreat, you can participate for two months, one month or at least a few weeks. You can do even just one week. I especially hope that this retreat will also be established in

Mongolia, since their main food is meat and so many animals are killed there every day. This practice is a great help in purifying that. After our temple in Mongolia has been built, I hope that thousands of people will attend mani retreats there. I would also like this retreat gradually to be established in other parts of the West as well.

This retreat also blesses the country where it is held and brings so much peace, happiness and prosperity to the land.

Even if you know the teachings on how to meditate on bodhicitta, you still need to receive the special blessings of the deity, Compassion Buddha. You receive these by doing the meditation and recitation we practice in the *mani* retreat. Therefore, recitation of OM MANI PADME HUM is one way to actualize bodhicitta–to transform your mind into bodhicitta and make your meditation on bodhicitta effective.

Generally, according to my experience, in my home Solu Khumbu in the Himalayas of Nepal, there are people who live their lives chanting OM MANI PADME HUM but have no idea of the three principal aspects of the path–renunciation, bodhicitta and the right view of emptiness–not even the words. Even though they can't read and don't even know the alphabet, they have great devotion to compassion and bodhicitta and live their lives reciting OM MANI PADME HUM. Such people are warm-hearted, very kind, very compassionate. This is proof from my own experience that reciting this mantra has the effect of transforming the mind into a good heart and compassion.

Without bodhicitta, you cannot cause all happiness for all sentient beings. You cannot do perfect work for all sentient beings, and you cannot achieve the complete qualities of the realizations and cessation, even for yourself.

Thus, everyone is most welcome to join the one hundred million OM MANI PADME HUM mantra retreat.

Colophon

Composed by Lama Zopa Rinpoche during a stay at Deer Park Buddhist Center, Madison, Wisconsin, USA, July 2000. Scribed and edited by Lhundup Damchö.

Friday, December 22 (A)

Morning: Second Mani Session

Thirty-five Buddhas practice

Before doing prostrations to the Thirty-five Buddhas, recollect impermanence and death, which is the nature of our life. Think very strongly that your death could happen at any time. Also generate a strong motivation of bodhicitta, even though you also generate a motivation of bodhicitta at the beginning of the sadhana.

Motivation for the mantra recitation

Before the recitation of mantra, I want to emphasize that it is very important to again make your bodhicitta motivation very strong. Of course we can think in many different ways to effectively transform our mind into a motivation of bodhicitta, but one way to do it is to think in the following way.

"The numberless hell beings, from whom I receive all my past, present and future happiness, all realizations and enlightenment, are the most precious and most kind ones in my life—I must free them from all their suffering and its causes and bring them to Compassion Buddha's enlightenment by myself alone.

"The numberless hungry ghosts, from whom I receive all my past, present and future happiness, all realizations and enlightenment, are the most precious and most kind ones in my life—I must free them from all their suffering and its causes and bring them to Compassion Buddha's enlightenment by myself alone.

"The numberless animals, from whom I receive all my past, present and future happiness, all realizations and enlightenment, are the most precious and most kind ones in my life—I must free them from all their suffering and its causes and bring them to Compassion Buddha's enlightenment by myself alone.

"The numberless human beings, from whom I receive all my past, present and future happiness, all realizations and enlightenment, are the most precious and most kind ones in my life—I must free them from all their suffering and its causes and bring them to Compassion Buddha's enlightenment by myself alone.

"The numberless asuras, from whom I receive all my past, present and future happiness, all realizations and enlightenment, are the most precious and most kind ones in my life—I must free them from all their suffering and its causes and bring them to Compassion Buddha's enlightenment by myself alone.

"The numberless suras, from whom I receive all my past, present and future happiness, all realizations and enlightenment, are the most precious and most kind ones in my life—I must free them from all their suffering and its causes and bring them to Compassion Buddha's enlightenment by myself alone.

"The numberless intermediate state beings, from whom I receive all my past, present and future happiness, all realizations and enlightenment, are the most precious and most kind ones in my life—I must free them from all their suffering and its causes and bring them to Compassion Buddha's enlightenment by myself alone.

"To do this, I must achieve Compassion Buddha's enlightenment; therefore, I'm going to do the meditation-recitation of Compassion Buddha."

Also, you can then specifically think, "Every single OM MANI PADME HUM mantra that I recite is for every hell being, every hungry ghost, every animal, every human being, every asura being, every sura being, every intermediate state being. Each OM MANI

PADME HUM that I recite is for the benefit of every single one of my most precious, kind mother sentient beings."

You can also dedicate each OM MANI PADME HUM you recite to the fulfillment of the holy wishes of the virtuous friend. You can dedicate each mantra for the holy wishes of the Compassion Buddha, His Holiness the Dalai Lama, to succeed immediately, especially His Holiness's important wish for the Tibetan people to have complete freedom in their own country as quickly as possible. You can dedicate as well for the government of mainland China to invite His Holiness the Dalai Lama to give teachings to all the millions of Chinese people and for there to be total religious freedom in China.

In addition, through the generation of loving kindness and compassion, of the good heart, may all wars and killing, famine, disease and all the other undesirable things that are happening in this world stop right now.

If any of your family members or friends have passed away through cancer, AIDS and so forth, also remember them and dedicate for them to achieve as quickly as possible the ultimate happiness of full enlightenment.

VISUALIZATION DURING THE MANTRA RECITATION

During the recitation of mantra, you can do the visualizations as mentioned this morning. Those who have received a great initiation have many meditations they can practice. You can first concentrate on divine pride, then on clear appearance and then put these two together, focusing single-pointedly on the clear appearance of yourself as the deity, as Compassion Buddha, with the deity's holy body. In the lower tantras, the particular term for this is *the transcendental wisdom of non-dual profundity and clarity*, whereas Highest Yoga Tantra has *the transcendental wisdom of non-dual bliss and voidness.*

Here, the transcendental wisdom of non-dual profundity and clarity means the mind focuses on the deity's holy body, but at the same time understands that it does not have inherent existence. There is the awareness that what appears to be inherently existent is not true. While that one mind is focusing on the deity's holy body, at the same time it has that understanding.

How to do this is described in some detail here in the text [pp. 98-99],[3] and you can do this meditation while reciting OM MANI PADME HUM. In addition, you can meditate on bodhicitta, using either equalizing and exchanging self with others or the seven techniques of Mahayana cause and effect. While reciting OM MANI PADME HUM, you can reflect on the extensive sufferings of others by following the lam-rim outlines and visualize them being purified of those sufferings. You can also meditate on equalizing and exchanging self with others, then practice *tong-len*, taking the sufferings of other sentient being upon yourself and giving them your own body, happiness and merits.

Very new people, who haven't previously attended lam-rim teachings, can visualize nectar beams being emitted from the front-generated Compassion Buddha, the embodiment of universal compassion. The compassion of all the buddhas, which embraces and never gives up you or any other sentient being, manifested in this form of thousand-armed, thousand-eyed Compassion Buddha to guide you and bring you all the different levels of happiness up to enlightenment. Like sunbeams, nectar beams—or just light—are emitted from Compassion Buddha and totally illuminate you, just as a light illuminates a dark room. And just as darkness is dispelled when you switch on a light, all your problems and all the causes of your problems—your negative emotional thoughts and negative imprints—are completely dispelled, completely purified. While you are doing this visualization, recite OM MANI PADME HUM.

If you have cancer, AIDS, or another sickness or any other problem, it is incidentally purified. Mental and physical problems are symptoms, or manifestations, of the negative karmas within you, and you have purified the causes of them, your negative emotional thoughts and the negative imprints left by them on your mental continuum. At the same time as you visualize doing this, chant OM MANI PADME HUM. Recite one or more malas as you purify yourself, then one mala as you purify your family members, then your friends, strangers, and especially your enemies.

Even if you don't know the lam-rim, even if you don't know in depth about the different levels of suffering that sentient beings experience, you can see that the world is full of problems. Those who haven't studied lam-rim can think of all the problems in the world. They can think of all the different sicknesses, of all the heavy sicknesses such as cancer, AIDS and multiple sclerosis, which have no cure or are difficult to cure. They can think of famine, wars and all the other problems that are happening right now. Some people, for example, are experiencing such heavy, suffocating relationship problems that they are mentally in hell.

Beams are emitted from Compassion Buddha to purify and liberate all those beings from all the sicknesses, famines, relationship problems, and the many other problems that they are experiencing. There are so many problems that you can think about. All those sentient beings are purified and liberated from all those problems and the causes of those problems: the negative emotional thoughts of anger, attachment and self-cherishing and the negative imprints left by them on the mind. All of them are completely purified.

Think extensively of all these problems and then recite OM MANI PADME HUM for the sentient beings who are experiencing them.

During the next part of the recitation, visualize that you receive all the qualities of the Compassion Buddha within you, especially the infinite compassion that embraces all sentient beings. You also receive omniscient mind, which can directly see the minds of all sentient beings and all the methods to bring them from happiness to happiness to enlightenment, as well as the perfect power to be able to reveal all these methods to them. You receive within you all the blessings of the infinite qualities of Compassion Buddha's holy body, holy speech and holy mind. After that, recite some more malas as you visualize that others also receive the blessings of the infinite qualities of Compassion Buddha.

When the group starts the mantra recitation, it might also be better and more helpful for the new people if it is done slowly. [Rinpoche chants OM MANI PADME HUM slowly, then moderately quickly, then very quickly.]

While you are reciting the mantra, check your motivation from time to time to see whether it is staying on the right track. If your motivation is not on the right track, if it is not a virtuous motivation but has become one of self-cherishing, attachment and so forth, transform it into the thought of benefiting other sentient beings. Remember, "What I am doing is for sentient beings," and transform it into a motivation of bodhicitta.

2

Friday, December 22 (B)

EVENING: FINAL MANI SESSION

DEDICATIONS

[Venerable Jinpa had just read out a dedication prayer requesting perfect human rebirths for various people who had died, including Venerable Dechen.]

I am not sure exactly when Venerable Dechen, one of the strict retreaters at Shiné Land, died—I think it was two or three weeks ago. She was a very strong practitioner who did a lot of practice, especially the preliminary practices. She suddenly passed away. They couldn't find the cause of her death, but I think that it was nothing that disturbed her mind.

"Due to the merits of the three times collected by me and those collected by others, may all those whose names have been mentioned here today, as well as all others who have passed away, be born in a pure land of Buddha where they can immediately become enlightened, or receive a perfect human rebirth in all their future lives, meet perfectly qualified Mahayana teachers, and by meeting the Mahayana teachings, achieve enlightenment as quickly as possible.

"May those who are now experiencing unimaginable suffering in the lower realms—where the suffering is so unimaginable that even a second of it is like eons of suffering—immediately be liberated from those sufferings and reincarnate in a pure land where they can quickly become enlightened. Or, by receiving a perfect human rebirth, may they meet the complete teachings of the Buddha, the Tibetan Mahayana teachings, and especially Lama Tsong Khapa's teachings, and be guided by a perfectly qualified Mahayana virtuous friend."

We can dedicate the next prayer to all the sentient beings who are sick or who have passed away, and especially to all those whose names were mentioned here. Recite "Prayer for Spontaneous Bliss" for all of them.

MANI PILLS

[During the Mani Retreat, each person was given a mani pill at the end of each mani session.]

These mani pills, which come from Dharamsala, have been blessed by His Holiness the Dalai Lama. Even though His Holiness may not have attended the blessing of the pills every day, His Holiness did come to some of the sessions and recited many prayers.

It is very good if the person who blesses pills is a bodhisattva or a yogi with actual realization of clear light and the illusory body. If a yogi with these realizations of the Highest Yoga Tantra path does the blessing, substances can be transformed and become extremely powerful. Here it is not just that. These pills have been blessed with many prayers by the actual Buddha of Compassion. In addition, many meditators who come down from the mountains, monks and lay people chant OM MANI PADME HUMs to bless these pills.

Mani pills usually multiply, though I don't know how this would be explained scientifically.

One Sera-je monk, the resident teacher at a Dharma center in Germany, went to Ladakh and organized the recitation of 100 million OM MANI PADME HUMs. They made mani pills during the retreat, and the pills multiplied. The people who had gathered there then developed so much devotion that they themselves started organizing the recitation of 100 million OM MANI PADME HUMs in their own areas. Actually seeing the pills multiply gave them so much faith and inspiration that when they went back to their own homes, they started retreats to recite 100 million OM MANI PADME HUMs.

There are different types of pills. The pills to develop wisdom are blessed with the meditation-recitation of Manjushri or other deities; due to dependent arising, taking the pills helps to develop wisdom. There are also long-life pills, which are blessed by hooking the essence of the holy body, holy speech and holy mind of those who have achieved the realization of immortality. Taking long-life pills is a condition that helps to prolong life. There are also pills for purification, which are blessed with the meditation-recitation of deities for purifying negative karma, such as Mitukpa (Immovable Buddha). It seems there is also a Mitukpa practice to make pills, which you then take for purification.

Here, the mani pills help you develop compassion.

THIRTY-FIVE BUDDHAS PRACTICE

I have some suggestions to make. When we do the Thirty-five Buddhas practice, as well as doing prostrations to each Buddha we should specifically recite the name of each Buddha. I strongly suggest that if you know the names by heart you *must* recite them. If you haven't memorized the names, what can be done? But if you have memorized the names, you *must* recite them. If only one person recites the names, only that person is purified. Reciting even the very first name, that of Guru Shakyamuni Buddha, purifies 80,000 eons of negative karma. Of course, listening to the recitation does plant seeds of enlightenment; but if you yourself don't actually recite the names at all, you don't purify all those many negative karmas. Therefore, if only one person recites and the rest don't recite, only that person gets purified.

We are doing prostrations to the Thirty-five Buddhas, but the main point is actually for you yourself to use your lips to recite so that all those many eons of negative karma are purified. I gave the example of the first name; in a similar way, by reciting each of the names once, you purify so many eons of negative karma. I'm not sure, but I think at different times here I have gone through the benefits of reciting the names of each of the Thirty-five Buddhas, explaining how many eons of different negative karmas are purified with each one.

I remember that when we were doing the Most Secret Hayagriva retreat at Vajrapani Institute, I asked everybody to memorize the names of the Thirty-five Buddhas during the retreat. I told everybody that by the time the retreat had finished they at least had to know all the names by heart. I don't think everybody tried, but some people definitely memorized the names during that time.

We spend our whole life neglecting all these unbelievably precious Mahayana practices and teachings, methods that are like atomic bombs in purifying all the heavy negative karmas we have collected during beginningless rebirths up to now, and then we die. In so many years, you have never memorized even the names of the Thirty-five Buddhas, and you will die without having memorized them. If you haven't memorized the names, you cannot recite the names while you are doing the prostrations, unless you use a tape-recorder to guide you, unless you take refuge in a tape-recorder. You have to put a tape-recorder as the *umze*, the chant-leader. That is very sad—very bad and very sad. Not to have memorized the names of the Thirty-five Buddhas after so many years is terrible; it's extremely lazy.

Of course, you need to see the benefit of doing the practice. Reciting well the prayer with the names of the Thirty-five Buddhas has the power to purify the five uninterrupted negative karmas, which are very heavy negative karmas. You don't have to experience the results of other negative karmas immediately; they can be interrupted by other lives, and then be experienced after one life or after many hundreds of lifetimes. But these five uninterrupted negative karmas (killing one's father, one's mother or an arhat, causing blood to flow from a Buddha and causing disunity among the Sangha) immediately, without the interruption of another life, cause one to reincarnate in the Unbearable Suffering State, the eighth hot hell, which has the heaviest suffering among all the hell realms. These heavy negative karmas are completely purified by reciting the Thirty-five Buddhas' practice well just once.

This is what Denma Lochö Rinpoche explained. I was wondering why there is no mention in Lama Tsong Khapa's life-story of his having done hundreds of thousands of prostrations to Vajrasattva, even though Vajrasattva is a very common practice in all four traditions; there is only mention of his doing many hundreds of thousands of prostrations with the Thirty-five Buddhas' names. When I asked Denma Lochö Rinpoche, this is what Rinpoche answered. There must be a special reason why Lama Tsong Khapa did so many prostrations to the Thirty-five Buddhas. And in the Gelugpa tradition, all the lineage lamas of lam-rim have done many hundreds or thousands of prostrations every day while reciting the names of the Thirty-five Buddhas.

This practice is *extremely* important. It is what we need. Even if we are going to live for a hundred years, the immediate thing we need to do is to purify our negative karma. Even if we have only five minutes left before we die, the immediate solution is to purify our negative karma, because it is our negative karma that causes us trouble, that causes a heavy death, and all the sufferings after death. Even in the future life when we're born as a human being, our life will still be filled only with problems. We will be born as a human

11

being, but we will spend our life experiencing sicknesses and many other problems, one after another. We won't be able to practice Dharma. The immediate solution, not only for our temporary happiness but especially for our ultimate happiness, is to purify our negative karma.

Of course there is an umze, a person who leads the prayer, but those who know the names by heart *must* recite them, so that by reciting each name you purify many eons of the different negative karmas you have collected. You will then have great success, great profit. Also, with your speech you will collect good karma, or merit. Otherwise, even though you are collecting merit with your body, you will be wasting an incredible opportunity to collect merit with your speech. By reciting the names of the Thirty-five Buddhas, you will collect so much merit and accomplish unbelievable purification.

Also, while it is very nice to have a space between the names of the Buddhas, and I understand that it gives you the chance to recite the name as you are prostrating to that Buddha, my suggestion is that you just keep on reciting nonstop. Keeping a space between the names gives you more time to purify as you are reciting the names of the Thirty-five Buddhas more times, but I suggest that you just go straight through the prayer without repeating the names and without a break between the names. Of course, when you do a certain number of prostrations, such as sets of a hundred prostrations, you can then repeat the same name over and over during each prostration.

By reciting Guru Shakyamuni Buddha's name once, you purify 80,000 eons of negative karma. If you recite the name three times, 240,000 eons of negative karma will be purified—that is unbelievable! We don't want the pain of a headache or toothache—let alone cancer—for one hour, or even one minute. The thought of purifying the suffering of 80,000 eons or 240,000 eons of toothache or cancer is very exciting. It is unimaginable. Each of the Thirty-five Buddhas' names is a wish-granting jewel that can liberate you from so much suffering and causes of suffering.

Reciting the prayer straight will also give more time for reciting OM MANI PADME HUM. All these little savings of time added together will help to give time to finish more mantras.

BLESSING THE VASE WATER

When blessing the vase [p. 133], even though the text says to recite the mantra 101 times, since we are having difficulty finishing the number of mantras, you don't need to recite that many. You can recite it just ten or fifteen times.

ADDITIONAL OFFERINGS

It would be good to have offerings of the seven royal signs, or king's reign, which are in the mandala offering; the eight auspicious signs; the eight substances and so forth around the mandala house. The idea is to have elaborate offerings.

According to some high lamas in Mongolia (or maybe in Amdo), there are also offerings of jewels and medicines in separate containers. The offering of medicine is for you and other sentient beings not to experience sickness. It is similar to when you fill a statue. In the throne of the statue, you put weapons for protection, medicines to guard against sicknesses, and food in the form of grain so that you do not experience famine. It is similar here. In one container you have five different grains, in another many jewels, in another medicine, and in another the five essences. I don't remember now what the five essences are—I will check. It would be good to have those offerings, and you can also have them during nyung-näs. In separate containers you have five medicines, five grains, five jewels, five scented smells and five essences.

There is a verse for offering all these five sets and dedicating to achieve Buddha's five kayas and five wisdoms. I think I have translated the verse before, but I will translate it again. There is also extra merit in making these offerings.

OFFERING A VASE

Also, in the offering of a vase [p. 126] that is done before the mandala offering and the praise, you pour water from the vase to purify the sentient beings of the six realms. The title says "offering a vase," but it is not just offering a vase. You pour just a drop of water out and visualize that the negative karma and suffering of the sentient beings of the six realms have been purified. It can be an offering of a vase, but the main point is to purify sentient beings' karma and delusions.

OFFERING MUSIC

You can make offerings of cymbals and drums at those places where cymbals are normally played and also in the section of the seven limbs where the sadhana talks about "holy flowers and garlands, cymbals and ointments..." [p. 65]. At that time you should also play music. That is what is normally done.

SEALING DEDICATIONS WITH EMPTINESS

After the prostrations, after looking at the three circles as empty, it is good to then dedicate the merits by sealing them with emptiness. Even though a dedication was done earlier, one might not have thought about its meaning. Just because the words have been recited doesn't mean the dedication has been done. Since one has to think about the meaning, dedicating again will be very helpful.

Look at everything—the creator, the action and the negative karma that is created—as empty, and with the continuation of that awareness, dedicate the merits. Even though the words you say are simply "Due to the merits of the three times collected by me and by others, may I achieve Guru Shakyamuni Buddha's enlightenment and lead all sentient beings to that enlightenment by myself alone," while saying them you should simultaneously have the awareness that all those things are empty. When you say those words, accompany them with the thought that all those things are empty. Whether or not you use the extra words to say that all those things are empty, you should have the awareness of emptiness while you are reciting the prayer of dedication. The awareness that they are empty should be present.

Right after you have sealed the three circles of emptiness, dedicate the merits to achieve enlightenment for sentient beings. While you are dedicating, the idea is to continue the understanding that they are empty.

Also, at the end of the sadhana where there is the verse "ge-wa di-yi..." [p. 166], you could do it in this way: "Due to all the merits of the three times collected by me and the merits of the three times collected by others, which are merely labeled, or which are merely imputed by the mind..." (When you think about this precisely, those merits that appear to be something real from their own side—or as Tsapel mentioned, "established from their own side"—are not there. It destroys the object of ignorance, the object that ignorance holds on to.) "...may the merely labeled I..." (When you say "merely labeled I" you should understand that there is no I that exists from its own side. That I that appears to exist from its own side becomes totally non-existent. It is supposed to be like that. It is not that there is a meditator-I and that that meditator-I is looking at a certain object, another I, and that I is what doesn't exist. That is wrong. The meditator-I itself is nowhere; it is *totally* non-existent. Not even a small part of that I that is not merely labeled by the mind exists.) "…achieve Buddha's (or Guru Shakyamuni Buddha's) enlightenment, (here, "Buddha's" enlightenment means the Thirty-five Buddhas' enlightenment,) which is merely labeled by the mind, and lead all sentient beings, who are merely labeled by the mind, to that enlightenment, which is merely labeled by the mind, by myself *alone*, who is also merely labeled by the mind."

So, at the end of the sadhana, instead of reciting "ge-wa di-yi…" you can recite this in English, by specially using the words of emptiness.

If dedicated for enlightenment, merits become inexhaustible. As you have heard during the lam-rim teachings or during the *Jorchö* (preparatory practices) commentary, when you dedicate even a small merit—such as having given one grain of rice to one ant—to achieve enlightenment, that merit becomes inexhaustible. You enjoy the result of having given that charity up to enlightenment. You enjoy the result of all the temporary happiness while you are in samsara, as well as all the realizations of the whole path to enlightenment and the infinite qualities of Buddha's holy body, holy speech and holy mind. And even after your enlightenment, you enjoy the result of liberating numberless sentient beings and bringing them to enlightenment. So, you enjoy the result, or benefit, of that merit even after you achieve enlightenment. You continuously receive the benefit or use the benefit to liberate numberless sentient beings and bring them to enlightenment.

However, if you don't seal the dedication of merit with emptiness, the merit is weakened and can be destroyed if heresy or anger arises afterwards. Here the meaning of "destroyed" is not that you make the merit completely nonexistent, as if completely burned. You cannot do that. But if heresy or anger arises, the effect it has is to weaken the merit. Pabongka Dechen Nyingpo explained in his advice to someone who had asked a question about dedication, that if, for example, you collect merit with a motivation of bodhicitta and also dedicate it to achieve enlightenment, it's like a huge mountain; however, if you dedicate the merits to achieve enlightenment but without sealing with emptiness, the merits can be destroyed, which means they become weaker or lessened. If there is a huge mountain, even though trucks transport many stones away from that mountain, there is still a mountain left; it's not the same as before, but still a mountain is there. It is like that with the merit. There is so much merit that it isn't completely destroyed, but it does become smaller if you don't dedicate the merits by sealing with emptiness. Generating heresy or anger weakens or lessens them. This implies that generating heresy or anger can destroy merits that are not dedicated to achieving enlightenment.

Therefore, sealing with emptiness becomes a very important practice, and this is the reason that at the end of the teachings I often dedicate the merits by applying the words of emptiness to each phenomenon. Even if one can't meditate, hearing the words of emptiness at least plants the seed to realize emptiness sooner or later. Even if one can't meditate precisely on emptiness, even reciting and just trying to think about the words still harms the ego; it still harms the ignorance that is the root of samsara. It becomes a preparation for eliminating that ignorance.

FRONT GENERATION

The way of guiding meditation is generally excellent, but I think that you could do the front generation faster. Just read straight through it, as it will give more time for recitation of mantra.

Generally, though, the way of guiding meditation is perfect—it's the way it should be done.

DEDICATION

At the end of the sadhana maybe the dedication verse "jang-chub sem-chog rinpoche…" is there in English [p. 163], but if that is chanted, you could think precisely about its meaning.

PRAYER OF ABIDING IN THE RETREAT

We should change the title "Prayer of the Fasting Ceremony" [p. 171]. It is probably in the translation in the book, but it is wrong. If you translate *nyung-nä* as fasting, it sounds as if the whole practice is simply fasting. Nyung-nä is not only fasting, though fasting is a part of the practice. *Nyung-nä* means "abiding in the retreat": *nyung* means "retreat" and *nä* means "abiding." We are abiding away from those activities that create negative karma.

In a nyung-nä, there is abiding in the retreat of the body, one part of which is fasting. But even the abiding in the retreat of the body is not just fasting. By visualizing your own body as the deity's holy body, you are also abiding in the retreat of the body. By visualizing the pure appearance of the deity's holy body, you are abiding in the retreat away from the ordinary, impure appearance of the body. And there are also other practices. Even the body abiding in the retreat is not just fasting.

There are also abiding in the retreat of the speech and abiding in the retreat of the mind, so how are you going to apply fasting to the speech or to the mind? That translation of *nyung-nä* is narrow and wrong; it should be changed to "abiding in the retreat."

BENEFITS OF THE MANI RETREAT

I think just that much for today. I think it is excellent to be doing such a practice; it is unbelievably fortunate.

At the end of the nyung-nä text there is an explanation of some of the benefits of reciting Compassion Buddha's mantra, but otherwise not much of all the extensive benefits has been translated into English.

This is such a wonderful time, especially doing practice to develop compassion and bodhicitta. Without compassion you can't have the realization of bodhicitta, you can't enter the Mahayana path, you can't achieve enlightenment, you can't achieve the infinite qualities of the holy body, holy speech and holy mind of Buddha. Without great compassion you can't do perfect work for sentient beings, bringing them to enlightenment. I mentioned this the other night when I arrived, but maybe it was difficult to hear so late at night....

Those who can make the time should come to the retreat. Even if you cannot come for all three months, you should come for some weeks—or at least for one week. If you do not give yourself the time, the freedom, to do this, it is very poor, very sad. Of course, it would be best to come for the whole time, until the end of the retreat, but if you cannot do that, while you can give yourself the time and the freedom, you should come for one month or for a minimum of one week. You should attempt to do this. If you have a family, of course it's not possible for all the family members, the whole assembly of parents and children, to come for the Mani Retreat, but maybe you could take turns. Do whatever you can, whatever days you can do. Give yourself the time to come again and again. Even if you cannot do one week straight, come again and again. Do at least one day, then come another day, then another day. At least come quite often in this way.

We should especially think of death. When the thought of death comes, when we remember death, there's nothing else that makes sense; everything else is total nonsense. When we think of death, so much of what we do in life doesn't make sense; it's all just nonsense. The only thing that makes sense is Dharma practice. Only Dharma will benefit us at the time of death and after death. The only thing that we can carry with us and can enjoy in our future life is Dharma—nothing else.

This practice of the meditation-recitation of the Buddha of Compassion will especially benefit us. Reciting OM MANI PADME HUM has merit as limitless as the sky. Even Buddha can never finish explaining the unbelievable purification and collection of extensive merit brought by reciting OM MANI PADME HUM.

This is a special means to develop compassion. Intellectual study alone cannot bring you the realization of compassion and bodhicitta. With the intellectual understanding, you then have to purify your mind and collect extensive merit. On the basis of those preliminary practices, you then receive this special deity's blessings by reciting OM MANI PADME HUM. It is through this that the realizations of great compassion and bodhicitta then come. Reciting OM MANI PADME HUM is one of the most powerful means of developing compassion and bodhicitta. Doing specific meditation on the Buddha of Compassion and reciting the mantra are like soil and water, the conditions that together enable a seed to produce a sprout, or like the pieces that are all put together to enable a clock or watch to show time. The mind works in a similar way. The preliminary practices and the meditation-recitation of Compassion Buddha persuade the Compassion Buddha's holy mind. Purifying negative karmas, or obstacles, and collecting extensive merit enable us to receive the blessings of Compassion Buddha, and through these blessings we then receive realizations. And the benefits of compassion are as limitless as the sky. After hearing the lam-rim and having studied it and also other teachings, we can understand the benefits of compassion. Compassion has limitless benefits for you and for all other sentient beings.

And I would like to mention something to the Sangha. Because there was intensive study before, of course you need a break. However, unless the Sangha need to go out to give Dharma talks or things like that, they should be the main people here doing the retreat, reciting the 100 million OM MANI PADME HUMs. Apart from those kind of activities, it is not permitted; the Sangha must do the retreat. That is one point that I want to mention. The Sangha must be the main ones to take responsibility for this retreat of 100 million OM MANI PADME HUMs. Except for special activities like giving Dharma teachings, the Sangha are not permitted. The Sangha *must* continue the retreat.

The lay people should also do as much as possible to fulfill this practice. This is the first time such a retreat has been done in the FPMT. I don't know whether other traditions such as the Kagyu or Nyingma have done such a retreat in the West, but this is the first time it has happened in the Gelugpa tradition. So, take responsibility for the retreat as much as possible.

At the end we will make an offering of this recitation to His Holiness the Dalai Lama, for all his holy wishes to succeed, especially his wish to spread Dharma and, in particular, for the freedom of Tibet. The retreat will also be dedicated for His Holiness to benefit all the people in mainland China by going there and, like the sun rising, bringing peace and happiness and spreading the Dharma. The retreat is not only for one's own enlightenment, but also for all these other purposes. As I mentioned earlier today at the beginning of the mantra recitation, it is also for world peace.

So, I'm extremely happy with those who have helped in the Mani Retreat that is happening here. Is it "Mani Retreat" or "Money Retreat"? "Mani" or "Money"? Maybe we will get some Money Retreat by the way. We're doing a Mani Retreat, but it will become a Money Retreat. Anyway, I'm just joking!

So, I think that's all. Thank you. Thank you very much.

3

Saturday, December 23 (A)

MORNING: *COMBINED JORCHÖ/LAMA CHÖPA PUJA*

GURU YOGA DEDICATION

[The following is inserted on p. 79 of *Combined Jorchö and Lama Chöpa Puja* as the first dedication in *Dedication Prayers*.]

"Due to all the past, present and future merits collected by me and the merits of the three times collected by others, may I, the members of my family, all the students and benefactors of the FPMT, as well as all other sentient beings, meet only perfectly qualified Mahayana virtuous friends." That is the first point.

"May I and all other sentient beings from our side be able to see them as only enlightened beings from their side." That's the second point.

The third point is, "May we do actions only pleasing the holy minds of the virtuous friends."

And fourth, "May we be able to fulfill the holy wishes of the virtuous friends immediately and in all our lifetimes from this second until enlightenment is achieved."

All our success, including enlightenment and liberating the numberless sentient beings and bringing them to enlightenment, depends on how well we are able to practice these four points in our daily life: meeting a perfectly qualified Mahayana virtuous friend; seeing them as only an enlightened being, not as an ordinary being; doing actions only pleasing the holy mind of the virtuous friend, which is extremely important and the most powerful means of purification; and fulfilling their holy wishes immediately.

This is a very important dedication in our daily life, especially at the end of guru yoga practice. This dedication should be done first and then chant "ge-wa di-yi..."as you have just done. What you have just done is excellent.

MAKING REQUESTS TO THE GURU

I think it would be good to recite the qualities of the guru [starts verse 43] in English, because it becomes a very important meditation on guru devotion, reflecting on the qualities of the guru. There are different general and particular qualities according to the Lesser Vehicle, the Mahayana, and then tantra.

It would be very nice if the same tune as "yön-tän jung-nä..." could be chanted, but with the words in English. The chanting is then there, but the meditation is also there. If the tune doesn't fit, other tunes could be used. It is a very important meditation, and it also contains the kindness of the guru.

When you begin chanting "kyö-ni la-ma..." [Verse 53], instead of starting immediately "kyö-ni la-ma..." it's good to begin "wo-o-o kyö-ni la-ma...." His Holiness Song Rinpoche often used to advise to start the chanting in this way. You start with "wo-o-o kyö-ni..." instead of starting straight with "kyö-ni...." I'm not sure that you start like this with every chant, but with most of them you do. In such cases as "kyö-ni la-ma..." it feels more fitting.

When there are three repetitions of "kyö-ni la-ma..." it is good to do the elaborate chanting first, as was done, rather than at the end; again, that is the proper way to do it. And when there are three repetitions, one of them can be done in English.

And it would sound nicer if the verse that comes at the end of the three repetitions of "kyö-ni la-ma..." [Verse 54] could be chanted more slowly. I remember that at Nalanda Geshe Jampa Tegchok used to chant this verse in a high voice and very slowly. It sounds beautiful when it is chanted slowly.

BODHISATTVA AND TANTRIC VOWS

When we take the bodhisattva and tantric vows [after verse 37], it might be helpful to also mention a motivation at that time, because it has some effect on the mind. Make a precise motivation that explains why the different vows are taken, but also gives other people insight or understanding.

"The purpose of my life is to free all sentient beings from all their sufferings and bring them to enlightenment. Therefore, I must achieve enlightenment. This is not possible without the bodhisattva vows; therefore, I'm going to take the bodhisattva vows."

When you motivate like this, it encourages you as to the importance of your practicing the bodhisattva vows, and it also helps make other people who have not taken bodhisattva vows aware of their special purpose.

And when it comes to the tantric vows, motivate in the following way. "Not just one but numberless sentient beings, who are the most kind and most precious ones to me, are suffering in samsara. To allow them to suffer for a day, or even a minute, is unbearable. Therefore, I *must* achieve enlightenment as quickly as possible. And since there is no other means to do this except by living in the tantric vows, I am going to take the tantric vows."

Motivating like this and then taking the tantric vows will remind you, as well as others who have taken tantric vows, of the importance of the tantric vows and tantric practice. It will also help those who haven't taken tantric vows to understand the importance of taking them.

MANTRA RECITATION

The first mantra [after verse 54] is actually one that combines Vajradhara, Lama Tsong Khapa and the root guru; all three are combined in that mantra. I think the usual mantra is OM OM AH GURU VAJRADHARA SUMATI KIRTI SIDDHI HUM HUM, where SUMATI is the Sanskrit term for "Losang" and KIRTI the Sanskrit term for "Dragpa." The reason for adding the root guru's name is to see that in essence the root guru is Vajradhara. We should not see the guru as somebody separate from Vajradhara, as that is an obstacle to realizations. In essence the guru is Vajradhara, and also Tsong Khapa. The root guru's name comes there to remind us of that meditation. For example, the mantra with the name of my root guru, His Holiness Trijang Rinpoche, from whom I received my first lam-rim teaching, on *Liberation in the Palm of Your Hand*, is OM AH GURU VAJRADHARA SUMATI KIRTI SUMATI GYANA SARVA SIDDHI HUM HUM, where SUMATI GYANA is His Holiness's name, Losang Yeshe, in Sanskrit.

I think I might have led the meditation on this here one or two times in the past. I'm not sure.

There is no doubt that *The Guru Puja* has to do with the extremely subtle consciousness; you are blessing your extremely subtle mind. Mind has three divisions: gross, subtle and extremely subtle. By doing these meditations of being oneness, you are actually blessing that extremely subtle wind-mind. The expression "five-colored beam" refers to the speech, which is also subtle wind. The meditation of oneness is like having poured milk into water or tea. Anyway, I will just mention that example; those of you who have received initiation will understand from what happens during initiation. It's a very important meditation, and that is the reason that the root guru's name is added.

You then recite the mantras of all the different deities.

Then, when you recite OM AH HUM, this is the integration of the vajra holy body, vajra holy speech and vajra holy mind of the numberless Buddhas. This is the integration of everything, with divine pride.

These are just bits and pieces, here and there. Anyway, it's fantastic—everything is fantastic!

RESPECTING HOLY IMAGES

I think that printing the timetable by superimposing it over a drawing of Thousand-armed Chenrezig might look nice, but it's disrespectful. In terms of karma, it is not good I'm telling you now so that it might help it not to happen again in the future. I think International Office might have done something similar some time ago; perhaps you got the idea from that—I'm not sure. I just thought to mention this.

Also, there are two or three mani stones on the path down to the office. These are not only Dharma, but also the most precious one, OM MANI PADME HUM, so they should be on a base. They can be there by the path, but they need to be on something high, not just on the bare ground.

So, I think that's it.

4
Saturday, December 23 (B)
MORNING: FIRST MANI SESSION

DEDICATIONS

"Due to all the past, present and future merits collected by me and the merits of the three times collected by others, may any sentient being just by seeing me, touching me, remembering me, thinking about me, talking about me (whether criticizing or praising), or dreaming about me never ever be reborn in the lower realms again. May they immediately be liberated from all disease, spirit harms, negative karmas and defilements, and may they achieve enlightenment as quickly as possible by actualizing the whole path, especially bodhicitta.

"Like Compassion Buddha and Lama Tsong Khapa, may I be able to offer extensive benefit to sentient beings from now on in all my future lifetimes by having the same qualities within me."

jam päl pa wo ji tar kyen pa dang
kün tu sang po de yang de zhin te
de dag kün gyi je su dag lob chir
ge wa di dag tam che rab tu ngo

"As the Buddhas and bodhisattvas of the three times dedicate their merits, and with the dedication they admire as the best, I dedicate all my merits in the same way.

"Due to all the merits of the three times collected by me and by others, may I, the members of my family, all the students and benefactors of the FPMT, and all other sentient beings, meet and completely actualize the teachings of Lama Tsong Khapa. May Lama Tsong Khapa's teachings spread in all directions and flourish forever."

OFFERING MUSIC

I was not saying that music should be offered just at that verse in the section of the seven-limb [p. 65]. You should offer music wherever it is normally offered.

FOOD OFFERING

[Rinpoche thinks that lunch is about to be served; in fact, there is another session before lunch.]

"I must free all sentient beings from all their suffering and bring them to enlightenment; therefore, I must achieve enlightenment; therefore, I'm going to practice the yoga of eating, making food offering and making charity toward all sentient beings."

All the food in the kitchen is purified in emptiness. A syllable BHRUM appears, which transforms into an extensive jeweled container. Inside it, an OM transforms into an ocean of uncontaminated nectar.

OM AH HUM (3x)

Offer the nectar to His Holiness the Dalai Lama, Compassion Buddha, as well as to all the rest of the gurus, Buddha, Dharma and Sangha, which includes the bodhisattvas, arhats, dakas and dakinis, and protectors. The essence of all of them is the root virtuous friend. There are numberless oceans of nectar, and we offer them to all the beings in the merit field, generating infinite bliss within them. Prostrate to all of them with your two palms together.

Offer numberless oceans of nectar to all the Buddhas, Dharma and Sangha of the ten directions.

Offer numberless oceans of nectar to all the holy objects—all the statues, stupas, scriptures and thangkas—of the ten directions.

Make charity of the nectar to every hell being, every hungry ghost, every animal, every human being, every asura being, every sura being, every intermediate state being. They all fully enjoy the nectar, and it liberates them from all their sufferings. They all become enlightened in the aspect of Compassion Buddha.

We have collected numberless merits with our motivation of bodhicitta; we have collected numberless merits by having made offering to all the merit field; we have collected numberless merits by having made offering to all the Buddhas, Dharma and Sangha. We have collected four times numberless merits by having made offering to all the statues, stupas, scriptures and thangkas. We have collected numberless merits by having made charity to all sentient beings. Also, we have collected so many times numberless merits by having prostrated with our two palms together to Buddha, Dharma and Sangha and all the numberless holy objects.

la ma sang gyä la ma chö
de zhin la ma ge dün te
kün gyi je po la ma te
la ma nam la chö par bül

"Due to all these merits collected by me and by others, may I, the members of my family, all the students and benefactors of the FPMT, and all other sentient beings never be separated from the Triple Gem, always collect merit by making offerings, and receive the blessing of the Triple Gem, which is every realization from guru devotion up to enlightenment, especially bodhicitta and clear light. May they be actualized within my own mind and in the minds of all sentient beings without the delay of even a second.

"Due to the merits of the three times collected by me and by others (which are empty), may the I (which is empty) achieve enlightenment (which is empty) and lead all sentient beings (who are empty) to that enlightenment (which is empty) by myself alone (who is also empty from its own side)."

Thank you very much. Enjoy the infinite bliss from the kitchen!

5

Saturday, December 23 (C)

AFTERNOON: THIRD MANI SESSION

MEDITATING ON THE SELF-GENERATION

During the sadhana, those who haven't received a great initiation of Compassion Buddha can still visualize Chenrezig in their heart and make all the offerings that are made to the self-generation Chenrezig to your heart-generated Chenrezig. It is the same.

Also, while those who have received a great Chenrezig initiation are doing the self-generation and making offerings to that deity, those who haven't received a great initiation can visualize Thousand-armed Chenrezig in front of themselves, then make all the offerings and do all the rest of the practice.

When there is a front generation, there is no question—you simply make the offerings to the front generation. But while the others are doing the practice of offering to themselves as the self-generation Compassion Buddha, those who haven't received a great initiation can do all those practices of offering either to Compassion Buddha in their heart or in front of them.

In this section [pp. 89-97] those who have received a great initiation of Compassion Buddha do the elaborate meditation on the six ways of generating oneself as the deity (if I translate the Tibetan term for this word by word, it might sound a little strange). This is the elaborate way of generating yourself as a deity in Kriya Tantra. There might also be a middle-length way, and the shortest way is to instantaneously generate yourself as the deity. The six graduated ways of becoming, clarifying and generating is the elaborate way.

However, while those who have received a great initiation are doing this practice, those who haven't received such an initiation, if they prefer, can visualize Thousand-armed Chenrezig in front of themselves, then do the single-pointed concentration on that front-generation Chenrezig. They can also do the practice of offering to that front generation, while the others are doing the practice of offering to themselves generated as Chenrezig.

Or, right after refuge and bodhicitta, you can visualize Chenrezig in front of you and immediately begin reciting the mantra. You can begin reciting the mantra either right after you visualize Chenrezig or after you have done the offerings.

DEDICATIONS

This time we can do the following dedication. "Due to all the past, present and future merits collected by me and the merits of the three times collected by others, from now on may whatever action I do with my body, speech and mind and whatever life I experience be most useful for other sentient beings. Whether I am up or down, happy or unhappy, healthy or unhealthy, whether I have cancer or don't have cancer, whether I have peace in my life or problems (such as relationship problems and so forth), whether I am rich or poor, whether I experience gain or loss, whether I receive praise or criticism from others, whether I am living or dying, or even born in the hell realms, may all my actions and life experiences from now on be most useful for other sentient beings, causing all sentient beings to achieve full enlightenment as quickly as possible.

"Due to all the merits of the three times collected by me and the merits of the three times collected by others, from now on in all my future lifetimes may I be able to offer extensive benefit, as limitless as the sky, to all sentient beings by having the same qualities within me as Compassion Buddha and Lama Tsong Khapa."

You can read "jam-päl pa-wo..." in English.

[The group reads:]
"Just as the brave Manjushri, and Samantabhadra, too,
Realized things as they are,
I also dedicate all these merits in the best way,
So that I may follow their perfect example."

Read the next verse as well—it's all one prayer.

[The group also reads:]
"I dedicate all these roots of virtue
With the dedication praised as the best
By the Victorious Ones of the three times,
So that I might perform the noble bodhisattva's deeds."

On the first morning of the Gelugpa meeting in Dharamsala, His Holiness the Dalai Lama recited the following dedication prayer, which was composed by Gendun Drub, the first incarnation of the Dalai Lamas. "First incarnation" means the first taking of a human form in the line of incarnation.

"Due to all the merits of the three times collected by me and by others, may the general teachings of the Buddha exist for a long time and, in particular, may the teaching of the glorious virtuous tradition of those wearing the yellow hat spread in all directions."

Think to actualize this completely within your mind and in the minds of the members of your family and of all the students and benefactors of the FPMT, as well as in the minds of all other sentient beings. May it spread in this way and flourish forever.

Mantras and meditations to multiply holy objects

I thought to mention the mantras that multiply the number of holy objects, such as tsa-tsas, that you make, though I think I have the oral transmission of only one of these mantras.

There are two practices for making tsa-tsas: one is in the collection of texts of the Lower Tantric College and the other is in the collection called "Ngülchu" of the great lama Ngülchu Dharmabhadra. I think I might have put together the tsa-tsa text that is available from those two texts, but I don't think that these mantras are in it.

I received this first mantra from His Holiness Chogye Trichen Rinpoche, His Holiness Sakya Trizin's guru.

You recite this mantra, with the visualization, to bless clay, plaster, cement or any other material that you are using not only to make small tsa-tsas, but also to build large statues or stupas. If you bless the clay, plaster or cement by reciting this mantra, you collect the merit of having made tsa-tsas, statues or stupas equal in number to the number of atoms of the material used to make the holy object. It's an unbelievable number! Even if you make a very small tsa-tsa, if you bless the clay or plaster with this mantra beforehand, since even a spoonful of clay or plaster contains millions and millions of atoms, you collect the merit of having made that many millions of tsa-tsas. If you bless the clay, plaster or other material that is used to make holy objects such as statues or stupas, you collect the merit of having made statues or stupas equal in number to the number of atoms in that material.

Reciting this mantra, which has the power to multiply merit, is a skillful means to collect extensive merit very easily, and in that way to achieve enlightenment quickly and easily.

So, this mantra is for blessing the clay, plaster or other material you are going to use to make a statue or other holy object. It is said to be the mantra of Buddha Vairochana—it is probably the long mantra of Buddha Vairochana.

OM NAMO BHAGAWATE / BEROCHANAYA / BHERBAHA RADZAYA / TATHAGATAYA / ARHATE SAMYAK SAM BUDDHAYA / TAYATA / OM SU GAKAYMAY SU GAKAYMAY / SAMAY SAMAYE / SHANDE DHANDE / ASAMA ROPAY / ANALAMBAY / TARAMBAY / YAKSHOWATE / MAHA TENZA / NIRA KULAY / NIRI WANI / SARWA BUDDHA / ARTIKATNA / ARTIKATAY / SOHA

That is the mantra, and the meditation is as follows. "Purify in emptiness by SVABHAVA." This means that by reciting "OM SVABHAVA SHUDDAH SARVA DHARMAH SVABHAVA SHUDDHO HAM," you purify in emptiness the clay, plaster, cement, bricks or other material you are going to use to make the statue or stupa. Then, while it is empty.... The Tibetan term is *tong-päi ngang-lä,* which means "while it is empty." *Ngang* means "while." If the translation is not done precisely and the "while" is left out, so that the phrase is translated as "out of emptiness" or "from emptiness," it appears as if you were looking at everything as empty before, but now it has suddenly become inherently existent. It seems as if when you actually visualize something, you have to visualize it as inherently existent. It doesn't make sense. You can see that when we actually try to visualize something, when it takes form, the idea of emptiness is gone; it becomes something else, and there is no connection with the previous idea of emptiness. That is a mistake. That way of translating or that way of thinking is wrong. The meditating on emptiness is correct, but after that there is no spontaneous awareness of emptiness, and suddenly everything is inherently existent, the total opposite. Whether you are visualizing yourself as the deity or the deity in front of you, if you are visualizing an inherently existent deity (or lotus or syllables), your meditation is wrong.

The awareness that everything is empty has to be continued, while it is taking form. Otherwise, it does not become the practice of Vajrayana, in which the one mind practices method and wisdom together. Your mind, that one mind of inseparable method and wisdom, is the meaning of vajra, and it becomes the vehicle, the *yana*, for you. Your mind becomes the vajra, inseparable method and wisdom, and that one mind, like a car or an airplane, takes you beyond samsara; it takes you beyond your delusions to enlightenment, so that is why it's called a vehicle. Your mind, that one mind of inseparable method and wisdom, is the vajra, and it becomes the yana that brings you to enlightenment quickly, even in this life. "In this life" is according to the lower tantras. According to Highest Yoga Tantra, it is "in a brief lifetime of the degenerate time," which means in even a few years.

Here, when you generate yourself as the deity, you first purify yourself in emptiness, looking at everything as empty, as it is empty. It is not that you are looking at something that is inherently existent as being empty. You are looking at that which is empty as being empty. That awareness then takes the form of a lotus, a syllable, or the holy body of the deity. So, there is the continual awareness that the lotus, the syllable or deity's holy body is also empty. While you are focusing on the lotus, you understand it is empty; while you are focusing on the syllable, you understand it is empty; while you are focusing on the deity's holy body, you understand that it is empty, that it doesn't have inherent existence. Until we become enlightened, everything always appears to us to be inherently existent, except for when we are in equipoise meditation after we have had the direct realization of emptiness and achieved the *arya* path.

However, even though there is an appearance of inherent existence, we understand that it is not true. Like this, we understand that the holy body of the deity doesn't have inherent existence.

According to Highest Yoga Tantra, one focuses on the deity's holy body and at the same time is aware that it does not have inherent existence. Focusing on the deity's holy body is the path of method, and understanding that it does not have inherent existence is the path of wisdom. The one mind practices method and wisdom. According to Highest Yoga Tantra, that becomes preparation for the unification of the illusory body and clear light. It becomes preparation for that path-time unification, and it also becomes preparation to achieve the result-time unification of the holy body of Rupakaya and the Dharmakaya.

Anyway, even if one does not have actual experience of the realization of emptiness, one can see things as an illusion or as a dream. One can at least use the words and understand it intellectually.

So, while it is empty, a lotus appears. On that is a moon disc, and on that the syllable BHRUM, which becomes huge piles of jewels. From the heart syllable of you, as the deity, beams are emitted to persuade the holy mind of Buddha Vairochana, the Victorious One of the Light, whose Sambhogakaya form is abiding in the realm of Ogmin. Inconceivable beams are then emitted from the heart of Buddha Vairochana and absorb into the clay, plaster, cement or other material, which then becomes of the nature of the transcendental wisdom of non-duality, the holy mind of all the Tathagatas.

Tathagata—or *de-zhin sheg-pa*, in Tibetan—means "gone-as-it-is." This means that Buddha's holy mind is directly seeing emptiness, "as-it-is," as phenomena are empty, without dualistic view, like having poured water into water. The Buddha's holy mind is forever inseparable, or immovable, from emptiness, so, in that way, de-zhin sheg-pa, Tathagata.

There is also a mudra. If this is the clay, plaster or other material that you are going to use to make holy objects, you hold your left hand like this. What's this finger called? [Ven. Ailsa: The little finger.] Little finger? Baby finger! Anyway, the mudra is like this. [Rinpoche touches his thumb and little finger together with the other three fingers stretched out straight and the palm facing up.] One hand faces down, the other faces up. [Rinpoche has his left hand below the material with the palm facing up and the right hand, in the same mudra, above the material with the palm facing down.] The mudra is like this, with the clay or plaster in between. Then, while doing the meditation of blessing, you recite the mantra.

I received this explanation from His Holiness Chogye Trichen Rinpoche. I was supposed to write it down and explain it to Colin [Crosbie] the last time I was here, but it didn't happen. It was supposed to happen last time, but it didn't. Anyway, this time it has happened.

There is also another mantra. It's a mantra not to die, which means we have to be in samsara forever. We have to choose either to die or to never die and be in samsara forever. No, I'm joking!

This is the mantra of rik-pa chen-mo, or great wisdom, Vimala Ushnika.

If you recite this mantra before you make a stupa—whether it's a small tsa-tsa stupa or a large stupa—you get the same benefit as having made ten million stupas. Reciting this mantra every day when you're building a large stupa has unbelievable benefits. Even if you recite this mantra just before you begin the stupa, you will get the same benefit as having built ten million stupas. This mantra is incredibly powerful. It has inconceivable, mind-blowing benefits. It is explained that by reciting this mantra and building one stupa, whether it's small or big, you get the same benefit as having built ten million stupas. That's unbelievable! If you were actually going to make ten million stupas, even small ones, imagine how many months or years it would take. If you were going to build ten million big stupas the size of Lama's stupa down there, imagine how many years, or maybe lifetimes, it would take. But if we recite this mantra when we start to build a stupa, we get the same benefits as having built ten million stupas without needing to undergo all the hardship.

Also, if you recite this mantra, any element—fire, water, air or earth—that touches your body becomes very meaningful. I would think that this also means that your own body becomes meaningful to behold, which means that by seeing or touching you, other sentient beings are liberated from their negative karma, the cause of the lower realms. Any one of the four elements, such as wind or water, that touches your body becomes blessed and has the power to liberate sentient beings; wherever the wind or water goes, the negative karma of any sentient being touched by it is purified. Any sentient being who sees or touches these elements is liberated from the lower realms; the benefit is double that of seeing or touching a stupa. I think this would also include the body of the person who recites this mantra; his or her body becomes meaningful to behold.

This mantra also purifies the five uninterrupted negative karmas, as mentioned before. These very heavy negative karmas are purified.

Also, you will develop tantric realizations. You will have a long life and wealth, will remember your past lives (and might also be able to see the future). You'll be protected from all harms and will become enlightened.

There is some advice from Droden Gyalwa-chö. I think this might be the name of one of Buddha's past lives. The term *Droden* is confusing. *Dro* means transmigratory beings and *den* means guide, but I'm not sure whether Droden Gyalwa-chö is a name of the Buddha or it means that after one becomes enlightened one then guides the transmigratory beings to enlightenment. I'm not sure whether the whole term *Droden Gyalwa-chö* is Buddha's name or it is simply talking about the function of the Buddha.

Anyway, Droden Gyalwa-chö said that it's good to recite this mantra on the day you are going to make stupas, whether it is a large stupa or even the very small tsa-tsa stupas. Tibetans make a lot of those tsa-tsas, where one tsa-tsa contains many small stupas, after people die and also for preliminary practices. You can recite this mantra every morning, especially while you are building a stupa, and you can also use it to bless the bricks, cement or any other material that you are going to put on the stupa. The whole point is that the more merit we are able to collect, the more easily and quickly we will be able to achieve enlightenment, which means that we will be able to liberate sentient beings from the suffering of samsara and bring them to enlightenment more quickly. That is the whole point of doing all these practices.

Whether you are repairing a stupa or making a very small stupa from clay, bricks or stones and whether you yourself are actually involved in the building or you are asking or hiring other people to build the stupa, if you recite this mantra 28,000 times before you build the stupa—whether you make a very small stupa the size of a fingernail (though some people's nails can be very long) or you make a stupa one *pag-tsä* high (there are different ways of measuring according to the Kalachakra and Abhidharmakosha systems, but I think one pag-tsä is eight *gyang-tags* and one gyang-tag is 500 arm spans [see p. 396 of *Teachings from the Vajrasattva Retreat*]; anyway, a pag-tsä is very long)—due to the power of mantra and single-pointedly reciting the mantra without distraction and with faith, after you have built the stupa, a scented fragrance similar to sandal-wood, musk or the divine incense of the devas will come from the stupa. And all your wishes and those of the other people who work on the stupa will be fulfilled. That is the main aim, of course. The main point is not that the stupa produces a scented smell but that all your wishes are fulfilled after you have made the stupa.

Also, you achieve all the collections of goodness, or qualities, which means you are able to achieve all the good things that you are wishing for. And if you had the karma to have a very short life, you will then have a very long life. At the time of your death, you will see a hundred million Buddhas, and the Buddhas will always con-sider you. Also, even after this life, in your next life, you will be born in a pure land of Buddha; you will receive the prediction about your enlightenment directly from Buddha, achieve the five types of clair-voyance and then achieve enlightenment in that pure land.

So, whether you are making a tsa-tsa stupa or a large stupa, if you recite as many mantras as possible, all your wishes and those of the others who are working on the stupa will be fulfilled. You will receive all these benefits.

I meant to advertise a long time ago that there is such a practice to do before you build a stupa, but it didn't happen. So, it might be helpful for those people who want to recite this mantra to achieve all that success, to succeed in all their wishes to have realizations, to benefit others and to serve the teachings of Buddha. It might help those who want to and can do this practice.

So, I think that's all. That's it for this time.

[Ven. Brian reminds Rinpoche that he hasn't actually given the mantra.]

Oh, I think I'll give it in the next Mani Retreat. Maybe I'll leave the mantra for next year's Mani Retreat. I'm joking.

These mantras are from the *Kangyur*, the Buddha's direct teachings, and I haven't yet received the oral transmission of the whole *Kangyur*. Those who have received the oral transmission of the *Kangyur* will have received these mantras, including the mantra I mentioned before, the one that if you recite before you build a stupa brings the same merit as having built ten million stupas.

I might have received the oral transmission of the first mantra from His Holiness Chogye Trichen Rinpoche, but I'm not a hundred percent sure. But I haven't received the oral transmission of this last one yet.

OM SARWA TATHAGATA / MALA BISHUDANI / RUDA BALAY / PRATI SANSKARA / TATHAGATA / DATU DARI / DARA DARA / SANDARA SANDARA / SARWA TATHAGATA / ATIKATNA ATIKATAY / SOHA

Some of the previous points I introduced, such as the path-time and result-time unification, are actually secret. Strictly speaking, not only do you need a great initiation of lower tantra to hear about them, but you also need a Highest Yoga Tantra initiation. But what to do? There is always a mixture of people, some who have received all the initiations and others who have never received initiation. However, if there is faith in the tantric teachings, that is better. Perhaps additional causes of hell have already been created, but maybe if some people benefited, then there's some hope.

Thank you so much.

6

Saturday, December 23 (D)

EVENING: FINAL MANI SESSION

PRAISE VERSE

It would be good to chant the short verse of praise [p. 102], so that the chanting also becomes part of the offering.

[Rinpoche chants the praise in Tibetan.]

It can be done even slower. It can be chanted, whether with this tune or another one, or it can be recited in English and then chanted.

MOTIVATIONS FOR MANTRA RECITATION

[Rinpoche blows his nose, then coughs.] That's it—that's the talk. Now it's finished....

I thought to mention this quite a few times, but it didn't happen. I think it would be good to change what is said before beginning the recitation of mantra. More or less the same thing can be said in each session, but it might be good to place the emphasis a little differently.

One time before you begin the mantra recitation you can use the motivation I gave yesterday. At another time you can use the following motivation.

"There are numberless kind and precious hell beings, and each mantra I recite is for every single hell being, for their temporary and ultimate happiness.

"There are numberless kind and precious hungry ghosts, and each mantra I recite is for every one of them, for their temporary and ultimate happiness.

"There are numberless kind and precious animals, and each

mantra I recite is for every one of them, for their temporary and ultimate happiness.

"There are numberless kind and precious human beings, and each mantra I recite is for every one of them, for their temporary and ultimate happiness.

"There are numberless kind and precious asura beings, and each mantra I recite is for every one of them, for their temporary and ultimate happiness.

"There are numberless kind and precious sura beings, and each mantra I recite is for every one of them, for their temporary and ultimate happiness.

"There are numberless kind and precious intermediate state beings, and each mantra I recite is for every one of them, for their temporary and ultimate happiness."

At another time you can use the following motivation.

"It is through generating the root of enlightenment, great compassion, that the realization of bodhicitta comes, which is the door to the Mahayana path to enlightenment. From bodhicitta then come all the Mahayana realizations: the six paramitas, the five paths, the ten bhumis, and also the realizations of the Highest Yoga Tantra path. The state of omniscient mind then comes, with the infinite qualities of Buddha's holy body, holy speech and holy mind. We are then able to do perfect work for all sentient beings, bringing them from happiness to happiness to enlightenment.

"Therefore, the most important thing in my life is to develop compassion, great compassion. This is of utmost importance. Just understanding the teachings on how to develop compassion is not sufficient. Even if we have all the information on how to develop compassion, we must still have the realization. For that, we must receive the blessing of the special deity of compassion by reciting the mantra that persuades the holy mind of the Buddha of Compassion. It is for this reason that I am going to recite the Compassion Buddha's mantra (or, do the meditation-recitation of Compassion Buddha)."

You can also motivate in this way before you recite the mantra. These two motivations could be done together or separately.

The next motivation is as follows.

"If I had the realization of great compassion, Mahayana compassion, the numberless hell beings, who are the most kind and most precious ones in my life and who are experiencing unbearable suffering, would be liberated from all that suffering and its causes and achieve enlightenment.

"If I had great compassion, the numberless hungry ghosts, who are the most kind and most precious ones in my life and who are experiencing unbearable suffering, would be liberated from all that suffering and achieve enlightenment.

"If I had great compassion, the numberless animals, who are the most kind and most precious ones in my life and who are experiencing unbearable suffering, would be liberated from all that suffering and achieve enlightenment.

"If I had great compassion, the numberless humans beings, who are the most kind and most precious ones in my life and who are experiencing the unbearable suffering of samsara and all the problems of human beings, would be liberated from all that suffering and achieve enlightenment.

"If I had great compassion, the numberless asura beings, who are the most kind and most precious ones in my life and who are experiencing unbearable suffering, would be liberated from all that suffering and achieve enlightenment.

"If I had great compassion, the numberless sura beings, who are

47

the most kind and most precious ones in my life and who are experiencing unbearable suffering, would be liberated from all that suffering and achieve enlightenment.

"If I had great compassion, the numberless intermediate state beings, who are the most kind and most precious ones in my life and who are experiencing unbearable suffering, would be liberated from all that suffering and achieve enlightenment."

"Therefore, I need to develop great compassion; therefore, I'm going to do the meditation-recitation of Compassion Buddha."

At another time you can do the motivation in this way.

Maybe I have not explained this in the best way. What I am trying to say is that if you have great compassion, it causes the realization of bodhicitta, and as I mentioned before, you then collect extensive merit. To achieve enlightenment you have to finish collecting extensive merit of wisdom and merit of virtue, or method. You need to complete these two collections of merit, and without them, you can't achieve enlightenment. What enables you to complete these two types of merit and to achieve the Dharmakaya and Rupakaya? (The merit of wisdom causes one to achieve the Dharmakaya and the merit of virtue to achieve the Rupakaya.) Great compassion. If you have great compassion, it happens; if you do not have great compassion, it doesn't happen. So, you can understand that by having great compassion, you are able to complete all the Mahayana realizations and achieve full enlightenment, which is the cessation of all the faults of the mind and the completion of all realizations. If you, the one person, have great compassion, you are able to liberate the numberless hell beings from all their suffering and its causes and bring them to enlightenment. If you, the one person, have great compassion, you are able to liberate the numberless animals from all their suffering and its causes and bring them to enlightenment. This is what happens if you, the one person, have great compassion. This is the benefit, as limitless as the sky, that you offer to others, to every single sentient being. You offer happiness to every single sentient being: the happiness of this life, the happiness of future lives and the ultimate happiness of liberation from samsara and enlightenment. You offer skies of benefit to every single sentient being, and that benefit comes from great compassion.

What I said previously may not have been clear—this is what I was trying to say.

You have to realize that doing this retreat is not like following the laws or regulations of a country, something each individual person does for his or her own benefit. It is for the peace and happiness of all sentient beings, as I mentioned just now. It is for world peace, for the happiness of this world. It is to pacify all the suffering and violence that is happening right now anywhere in the world.

As well as this, as I have mentioned quite a few times, this retreat is for His Holiness the Dalai Lama's wishes to be fulfilled, especially his wish for the complete freedom of the Tibetan people. It is also for the top people in mainland China to change their minds, totally devote themselves to His Holiness and invite His Holiness to China. The majority of the people in the world are Chinese, and this retreat is for the many millions of them to have peace and happiness in their lives, like the sun shining, by hearing His Holiness's teachings.

These are our particular purposes for doing this retreat; we are dedicating the retreat in this way.

Also, we will make an offering to His Holiness the Dalai Lama of this retreat. This is a way from our side to repay His Holiness's kindness. Even our doing this practice of reciting 100 million OM MANI PADME HUMs has happened because of His Holiness. As I mentioned before downstairs, without His Holiness we wouldn't have met Buddhadharma. It would not have been possible for the Buddha's teaching to come to the West, so we wouldn't have met Buddhadharma and whatever practice we have done since we met Buddhadharma—the sutra practices of renunciation, bodhicitta, emptiness and so forth, and also the tantric practices—which have made us so much closer to enlightenment, wouldn't have happened. None of these advantages that we have gained through these years would have happened. Our life would have been totally empty, totally ignorant. We have taken a human body, not a pig's body, but if we hadn't met Buddhadharma, we would be no different from a pig. Even though we would live in a more sophisticated, more expensive house than a pig, it would just be an external difference; internally we would be the same as a pig. If we hadn't met Buddhadharma, there would not be the slightest difference between our life and that of a pig.

That we have met Buddhadharma is totally by the kindness of His Holiness the Dalai Lama and of the Tibetan people, who protected and preserved the Buddhadharma for so many years in Tibet. So that Buddhism could be preserved purely, Tibetans didn't allow any other country to come in to develop Tibet materially and economically. They put all their effort into preserving the Buddha's teachings purely. And they were not just scholars but actually practiced the Buddha's teachings and achieved realizations and enlightenment.

The Tibetans preserved the Buddhist teachings for many years, not just in libraries or on bookshelves in their houses, but in unstained learning, practice and experience. It is because they preserved the teachings that we now have the chance to learn them. The reason that we now have the chance to learn from Geshe Tashi

Tsering is because the teachings were preserved in that way. If the teachings had been preserved just in books, with no people studying and practicing them, we wouldn't now have the chance to learn them.

Therefore, this retreat is also dedicated for the Tibetan people to achieve total freedom.

You can also dedicate for other countries. I already mentioned at the beginning that this retreat is dedicated to the resolving of all the violence and other problems in the world, so that includes the many other countries that are experiencing so much suffering. If you have a particular country in mind, you can also dedicate for that country.

Benefits of reciting six million manis

Another point is that if you are able to recite six or seven million OM MANI PADME HUMs, you can become a great healer. You then have the power to heal various sicknesses, as well as the ability to make rain or to stop it. After you have done that number of mantras, if you recite mantras to bless water or some other substance or just blow with your breath, you have much power to heal.

A text by Padmasambhava explains the various problems that you can solve. If you have recited six or seven million mantras, your activities become powerful; your various activities of peace, increase, control and wrath are certain to help others. This is not the main aim of the retreat, but it comes about incidentally that you can do these things to benefit others.

Remembering death

Every day here we hear the names of people who have died, including those of FPMT students. Even though we believe that we are going to live for a very long time, this life can change at any time.

Every morning when we wake up we have this wrong concept that we're going to live for many years. We even have this concept the moment before the car accident that kills us. Five minutes before the car accident, we have this concept that we're going to live for a long time. Even though we are going to die five minutes later, we're still confident that we're going to live a long time. This concept is there, even a few minutes before our death. So, this mind is cheating us.

I might have mentioned this story in the past. One young Japanese man died in Santa Cruz some years ago. When he found out that he was going to die (I don't know whether it was from cancer or something else), he got very angry, because he thought that the world had cheated him, deceived him. In some ways this was an intelligent way of thinking. He blamed the outside world, but he should actually have blamed his wrong concepts, the concepts of permanence and attachment. He didn't know that the blame should have gone on his delusions, on his wrong concepts. Because he didn't know Dharma, it appeared to him that the world had cheated him.

There are only a few words more, then it's finished....

This young Japanese man thought that the world had cheated him. When impermanent phenomena appear to you to be permanent and you believe it to be true, it cheats you. When things appear to you to be inherently existent, not merely labeled by mind, and you apprehend it to be true, it is cheating you at that time. If you don't believe it, however, it cannot cheat you. The problem is that in our daily lives, the second that we apprehend it to be true—for example, that the I is real, as it appears to be real, in the sense of existing from its own side—or as Tsapel said, "established from its own side"—the second that we believe in that, we are cheating ourselves. At that time it is actually your wrong concept, your ignorance, that is cheating you, so you are deceiving yourself.

It is useful to think that all these phenomena, including the I and all the sense objects, appear to you as not merely labeled by mind, even though they *are* merely labeled by mind. All these things appear as something other than what is merely labeled by mind. They should appear as merely labeled by the mind, but that doesn't happen. Even though that's the reality, it doesn't appear to us this way but as the total opposite, as not merely labeled by mind. Actually, it's useful to think that all these inherently existent appearances are illusions, or hallucinations, that are cheating you. To think in that way is a powerful practice.

I think in some ways the Japanese boy was quite intelligent, but because he didn't know Dharma, he got angry at the world. When he suddenly discovered death, which he had never thought about before, he found this experience frightening, something that he didn't want.

So, such a death can happen to us any day, any moment. Even if we don't have cancer or AIDS, it doesn't mean that they are going to live for a long time. It is not that not having cancer or AIDS means that we are going to live for a long time. Life is filled with obstacles. From within our mind there are so many obstacles, all the delusions and all the past karmas that are the causes of untimely death, and then because of them, there are also many external conditions for death. Life is filled with conditions for death. And even though food, medicines and even operations are meant to prolong our lives, many times they don't work.

Therefore, we really need to pay a lot of attention to this point. As I mentioned last night, the whole conclusion is that we need to purify our negative karma. That is the urgent practice, and any negative karma can be purified with OM MANI PADME HUM.

DEDICATIONS

The dedication for this session is, "Due to all the past, present and future merits collected by me and the merits of the three times collected by others, wherever I am—in whichever universe, world, country (such as here in Australia), area—just by my being there in that universe, world, country, area, may all the sentient beings there never ever be reborn in the lower realms again. May they immediately be liberated from all disease, spirit harms, negative karmas and defilements, and may they quickly achieve enlightenment by actualizing the whole path, especially bodhicitta.

"May all those with sicknesses in the universe, world, country, area where I am immediately be cured. May those who are suffering from poverty be able to have wealth. May those who have relationship problems find much peace, happiness, loving kindness and compassion. May those who are blind be able to see. May those who are lame be able to walk. May those who want to find a spiritual guru immediately be able to find a perfectly qualified guru. May those who need teachings immediately be able to receive teachings. May those who want to do retreat be able to get the time and all the necessary conditions to do so. May those who have much difficulty in their lives because of depression and whom no one can help immediately, without the delay of even a second, be healed, and may their hearts be filled with joy and peace. May those who are dying and are terrified of death immediately find peace of mind. May everyone's wishes for happiness be achieved in accordance with the Dharma."

In one of the sessions, you can dedicate for your life to be beneficial in numberless ways to sentient beings, like the compassionate white lotus; for you to bring skies of benefit to sentient beings. There is a story about the compassionate white lotus. I'm not sure, but I think it could be a manifestation of Buddha. Anyway, wherever it grows the compassionate white lotus brings incredible peace and happiness to all the living beings in that place.

Also do the Manjugosha and Samantabhadra dedication.

[The group recites:]
"Just as the brave Manjushri, and Samantabhadra, too,
Realized things as they are,
I also dedicate all these merits in the best way,
So that I may follow their perfect example.

"I dedicate all these roots of virtue
With the dedication praised as the best
By the Victorious Ones of the three times,
So that I might perform the noble bodhisattva's deeds."

This dedication is a simple prayer but it is regarded as very important because it contains all the extensive prayers of the bodhisattvas. That is why it is normally recited at the end. Everything that is contained in The King of Prayers, the bodhisattva Samantabhadra's prayer, is in this prayer. This is the abbreviated way of doing that prayer. You are dedicating the merits to be able to benefit sentient beings like those bodhisattvas.

The last prayer is to dedicate for Lama Tsong Khapa's teaching. Tonight you recited the extensive prayer for the spread of Lama Tsong Khapa's teaching, but generally at the very end you can dedicate to meet Lama Tsong Khapa's teaching. There is a prayer written in Tibetan, but you can do it in the following way. "Due to the merits of the three times collected by me and the merits of the three times collected by others, may I, the members of my family, all the students and benefactors of the FPMT, everyone who comes to Chenrezig Institute and to this Mani Retreat, as well as all other sentient beings, be able to completely actualize the whole stainless teaching of Lama Tsong Khapa, the unification of sutra and tantra, in this very lifetime. May Lama Tsong Khapa's teaching spread in all directions and exist forever, and may I be able to cause this to happen by myself alone."

You can do this dedication or one of the various prayers to meet or to spread Lama Tsong Khapa's teaching. You can do it either in Tibetan or English. However, the essence is for you, the members of your family, all the students and benefactors and so forth to actualize Lama Tsong Khapa's teaching and for it to spread in all directions and to exist for a long time.

Every tradition—Sakya, Kagyu, Nyingma—recites a prayer at the end for the spread of that tradition's teachings. It's the normal thing to do. But here there is extraordinary purpose in dedicating for Lama Tsong Khapa's teaching. It is not just because it is your tradition; there are additional reasons, but you will know the additional reasons only by studying Lama Tsong Khapa's teachings and then studying other teachings. You will then know why it is so important to pray to meet Lama Tsong Khapa's teachings.

A lama asked, I think, Panchen Losang Chökyi Gyaltsen, who composed *Lama Chöpa*, whether he could be born in Amitabha Buddha's pure land. Panchen Losang Chökyi Gyaltsen said, "Yes, yes, you can be born in the pure land of Amitabha Buddha." I don't remember exactly, but I think the lama then asked whether he would meet Lama Tsong Khapa's teaching again. Panchen Losang Chökyi Gyaltsen then said, "No. To meet Lama Tsong Khapa's teaching is difficult, but to be born in Amitabha's pure land is very easy. You can do that, but you cannot meet Lama Tsong Khapa's teaching."

According to many lamas, there are no tantric teachings in Amitabha's pure land. Therefore, even after you are born there, you have to pray to be born back in this world where we are now, the southern continent, where tantric teachings exist, so that you are able to practice tantra and achieve enlightenment quickly. There are many human worlds: the eastern continent, southern continent, western continent and northern continent. However, only the human beings of this world, of this southern continent, can achieve enlightenment within one life. Beings who can achieve enlightenment in one life have two characteristics: they can only be human beings, and not just any human beings, but human beings only from this southern continent where we are now. So, if we practice correctly we can achieve enlightenment in one life.

Because tantric teachings exist here now, even beings born in the pure land of Amitabha pray to be born here so that they can practice tantra and achieve enlightenment. This might be the explanation as to why Panchen Losang Chökyi Gyaltsen told the lama that it would be very difficult for him to meet Lama Tsong Khapa's teaching again, but that he could be born in the pure land of Amitabha Buddha.

It is only by studying Lama Tsong Khapa's teachings that you can find out for yourself why they are so precious. Lama Tsong Khapa's lam-rim teachings have the clearest explanation of the unification of emptiness and dependent arising, of the extremely subtle dependent arising that is the view of the Prasangika school. Lama Tsong Khapa has the clearest teaching on those extremely subtle points, as well as the clearest explanation of the points of calm abiding, such as subtle sinking thought. Also, in tantra, Lama Tsong Khapa gives the clearest explanation of how to achieve the illusory body, and so on and so forth. Many of Lama Tsong Khapa's explanations in sutra and tantra are very special ones. Therefore, it's very important at the end to dedicate to meet Lama Tsong Khapa's teaching. Tonight we did the extensive prayer, but at the end of the other sessions we should also dedicate to meet Lama Tsong Khapa's teaching.

So, that's all. I think that if I continue you are going to have nightmares. So, good night.

7
Sunday, December 24 (A)
MORNING: SECOND MANI SESSION

CALLING THE LAMA FROM AFAR

I thought to do the short *Calling the Guru from Afar* [p. 17]. Those who like to chant in Tibetan can chant it in Tibetan and those who like to read in English can read it in English—or you can do both.

Visualize your root virtuous friend, with the understanding that he is one with all the Buddhas.

[Rinpoche very slowly and beautifully chants the abbreviated *Calling the Lama from Afar.*]

"Please grant me blessings not to give rise to heresy for even one second toward the holy actions of the glorious guru, and with the devotion that sees whatever action the guru does as pure, may I receive the blessing of the guru in my heart."

You can see whether you can fit the English words to the chanting.

WHAT TO THINK ABOUT DURING THE MANTRA RECITATION

Those who have studied, read or heard the lam-rim have some idea of the extensive sufferings of the beings in each realm: the hell beings, hungry ghosts, animals, human beings, asuras, suras and intermediate state beings. All the sufferings are explained in detail in the lam-rim, so that you can meditate on them easily but extensively. Since the lam-rim and the sutra teachings explain the sufferings in detail, you have the general idea of how to reflect on them and develop strong compassion for those beings while you are reciting the mantra. You can also use the motivations that I gave the other day.

Those of you who have come to join the retreat and recite OM

MANI PADME HUM but haven't studied the lam-rim, the basic teachings that are the essence of the Buddhadharma, and have no idea of the bodhicitta meditations, need to do something else, in accordance with your capacity. Of course, you can reflect on all sentient beings and wish to free them from all suffering and its causes and bring them happiness. Then, in regard to happiness, you can think to bring all sentient beings not only temporary happiness but especially ultimate happiness, and within the category of ultimate happiness, bring them not just liberation from the suffering of samsara but the sublime happiness of full enlightenment.

It is also good to ask yourself, "Why do I have to do this?" There are two reasons. One very important reason is that sentient beings do not want suffering and want happiness. The other reason is that this is the purpose of your life. It is for this purpose that you put so much effort into surviving in every hour, every minute, of your life. The conclusion is that there are two reasons: this is what sentient beings need, so you should help them; and this is the meaning of your life.

You then think of as many sufferings as you can that are happening in the world. Think of all the wars that are happening right now in different countries. Then think of all the problems experienced by individual people. Think of all the cancer and AIDS. Millions and millions of people are experiencing cancer, AIDS and other sicknesses. Think of those who are in hospital experiencing various sicknesses. Think of those who are having heart attacks right now. Think of those who are in comas. So many people are having operations right now, and it's unsure whether they are going to survive or die today. Also, think of all the sick people at home. Then think of the people experiencing poverty, famine and unemployment. Reflect on all those things.

There are so many who are suffering. Even if you haven't studied Dharma, you know of so many problems that the world is experiencing or that individual sentient beings are experiencing. There are oceans of problems just among human beings. There are so many that you can think about. Even if you have never studied or meditated on lam-rim or read Dharma books, you know of so many sufferings that people are experiencing.

Reflect also on the sufferings of animals, those that you can see, that you remember or that you know about. Wish to free them from all those problems and for them to never ever experience problems again, which is the ultimate happiness of liberation. Think, "To bring them all temporary and ultimate happiness, I'm going to do the meditation-recitation of Compassion Buddha."

I am talking here particularly for new people. Of course, those who have studied and know the lam-rim can meditate very deeply and elaborately following the lam-rim outlines, which include all these sufferings. There is so much that you can meditate on.

To reflect on the various problems is very effective, even for those who know lam-rim, because when you think of the sufferings of other people, you've got to do something. And what are you going to do? At the very least, through meditation, you can purify them of the causes of their suffering and pray for them, and the most extensive benefit that you can offer others is to develop compassion within you for all sentient beings. You recite the mantra for that purpose.

Here I am explaining particularly for those who haven't studied Buddhism. Think of the various problems that you know. You don't need religious faith to do this. You don't need religious faith to understand the suffering of somebody with cancer. You know how many people are dying from cancer and from AIDS. The world is full of problems, and you see this every day on TV and in the newspapers. You can do the meditation for the benefit of all the people who are suffering, and also for you yourself to develop compassion.

This makes it easy for those who have never heard lam-rim teachings or have no idea about Buddhism. They then having something they know that they can think about.

Also, if you can't concentrate well or are falling sleep, it might help to have a lam-rim book in front of you to read. With your mouth you can recite the mantra while you read the lam-rim text. Your mouth chants OM MANI PADME HUM, but you read Dharma texts on whichever lam-rim meditation you want to do. It then becomes very rich, very meaningful.

Also, it might be helpful to have some idea of which meditation you are going to do, "This session I'm going to do this meditation and that session I'm going to that meditation." Make a program of meditations for the different sessions. Because you then have something to think about, there's no restlessness. Because your mind is set up with a lam-rim meditation, you do not become restless. Also, instead of your mind being distracted, your recitation of mantra becomes rich and meaningful because you are accompanying it with lam-rim meditation.

Or you can first start with the common meditation that is mentioned in the text [p. 105], sending beams to purify and enlighten all sentient beings and then making offerings to all of them. You can then meditate on the divine pride of yourself as Chenrezig and on clear appearance. At the same time look at yourself as Chenrezig, in the aspect of the deity's holy body, as an illusion; it appears to be inherently existent but it is not true. You can always begin each session with this, then do other meditations. Or you can do different meditations in each session. This makes the mantra recitation much more enjoyable, as there's so much to do that you don't become restless. It also helps to stop you from falling asleep.

I don't want my talking to become the session. We should at least recite a few mantras, a few syllables....

Food offering

First generate the motivation: "The purpose of my life is to free all sentient beings from all their suffering and its causes and bring them to enlightenment; therefore, I must achieve enlightenment; therefore, I'm going to practice the yoga of eating, making food offering and charity to sentient beings."

As we've just done the sadhana, you yourself are Chenrezig. All the food in the kitchen is purified in emptiness. (You can recite "OM SVABHAVA SHUDDAH SARVA DHARMAH SVABHAVA SHUDDHO HAM" or simply purify it in emptiness.) Then, while it is empty, your wisdom understanding emptiness is transformed into an extensive jeweled container, inside of which is an OM.

You have to understand the reason for visualizing OM. OM is made up of three sounds: "AH," "O" and "MA," which symbolize Buddha's holy body, holy speech and holy mind. You can now understand the way the blessing is done. The OM manifests in uncontaminated nectar, which in this way is blessed in the essence of Buddha's holy body, holy speech and holy mind. Actually, it manifests in numberless oceans of uncontaminated nectar.

If you have visualized the merit field surrounding Compassion Buddha—all the direct and indirect gurus, buddhas and bodhisattvas, Dharma protectors and so forth—they are all included in the Buddha, Dharma and Sangha.

Make offering of numberless oceans of uncontaminated nectar to His Holiness the Dalai Lama, with strong recognition that the essence is your root virtuous friend. Generate infinite bliss within them. Put your palms together and prostrate to them.

Make offering of numberless oceans of uncontaminated nectar to all the Buddha, Dharma and Sangha of the ten directions, imagining that their essence is your root virtuous friend. Generate infinite bliss within them. Prostrate to all of them.

Make offering of numberless oceans of uncontaminated nectar to all the statues, stupas, scriptures and thangkas in all the universes in the ten directions, imagining that their essence is your root virtuous friend. Generate infinite bliss within them. Prostrate with your palms together to all of them.

Make charity of numberless oceans of uncontaminated nectar to every single hell being, every single hungry ghost, every single animal (including the ants), every single human being, every single asura being, every single sura being, every single intermediate state being. They all fully enjoy the nectar and are liberated from all their suffering, including its causes. They all become enlightened in the aspect of Compassion Buddha. Visualize every hell being, hungry ghost, animal, human, asura, sura and intermediate state being as Compassion Buddha.

We collected limitless skies of merit—or good karma, the cause of happiness—with our motivation of bodhicitta. We collected limitless skies of merit by offering to all the beings in the merit field, with Compassion Buddha, Guru Avalokiteshvara, as the principal figure. We collected limitless skies of merit by offering to all Buddha, Dharma and Sangha of the ten directions. We collected four times limitless skies of merit by offering to all the stupas, statues, scriptures and thangkas of the ten directions. We collected seven times limitless skies of merit by making charity to all the sentient beings. (The hell beings are numberless, the hungry ghosts are numberless, the animals are numberless and so forth, so we created seven times numberless merits.)

"Due to all these merits, and the past and future merits collected by me and all the merits of the three times collected by others, may I, the members of my family, all the students and benefactors of the FPMT, as well as all other sentient beings, never be separated from the Triple Gem, always collect merit by making offerings, and receive the blessing of the Triple Gem, which is all the realizations from guru devotion up to enlightenment, especially bodhicitta and clear light. May all these realizations be actualized within my own mind and in the minds of all sentient beings without the delay of even a second."

Here, because we've collected so many times limitless skies of merit, we should dedicate again in the following way. If we don't dedicate the merit, it can be destroyed by our generating heresy or anger. An atomic bomb can harm the animate and inanimate world, killing many millions of people, but our heresy and anger are much more destructive. An atomic bomb is nothing when compared to the danger from our negative thoughts of anger and heresy.

"Due to all the past, present and future merits collected by me and the merits of the three times collected by others (which exist but do not exist from their own side), may the I (who exists but does not exist from its own side) achieve Compassion Buddha's enlightenment (which exists but doesn't exist from its side, which is empty) and lead all the sentient beings (who exist but do not exist from their own side, who are empty) to that enlightenment (which exists but does not exist from its own side, which is empty) by myself alone (who exists but doesn't exist from my own side, who is totally empty)."

I left out the chanting—the prayer should be done before the dedication.

la ma sang gyä la ma chö
de zhin la ma ge dün te
kün gyi je po la ma te
la ma nam la chö par bül

Yesterday I did the offering too early—I thought it was the last session before lunch.

8
Sunday, December 24 (B)
AFTERNOON: THIRD MANI SESSION

DEDICATIONS

"From now on, whatever action I do—eating, sleeping, walking, sitting, working and so forth—and whatever life I experience—up or down; happy or unhappy; healthy or unhealthy; whether I have a life-threatening sickness such as cancer or don't have any sickness; whether I have problems in my life, such as relationship problems, or have no problems; gain or loss; rich or poor; whether I receive praise and people like me or I receive criticism and people are negative toward me; living or dying, and even if I am born in the hell realms—the main purpose of my life is to be beneficial to other sentient beings. Therefore, may whatever I experience in my life from now on be most useful for other sentient beings. And what is the most useful thing? That which causes all sentient beings to achieve enlightenment in the quickest way possible. From now on, may all my actions and experiences in life become the cause for all sentient beings to achieve enlightenment as quickly as possible."

Now read "jam-päl pa-wo…" in English. [Group reads "Just as the brave Manjushri…bodhisattva's deeds." (p. 79) in *Combined Jorchö and Lama Chöpa Puja*).]

"Due to the merits of the three times collected by me and the merits of the three times collected by others, may I, the members of my family, all the students and benefactors of the FPMT, as well as all other sentient beings, meet and actualize the complete teaching of Lama Tsong Khapa, the unification of sutra and tantra, in this very lifetime without the delay of even a second. May this teaching spread in all directions and flourish forever, and may I cause all this to happen."

So, thank you very much. When you finished, I had just begun my session. So now I have to finish....

MANTRA RECITATION

The reason that after chanting OM MANI PADME HUM slowly, I then recite it a little more quickly and then very quickly is because I heard that some very new people were having difficulty in reciting the mantra. It is just to give you some idea of the way to chant OM MANI PADME HUM, and it is actually meant to be recited together.

Of course, strictly speaking, as mentioned in retreat instructions, mantra recitation should be free from eight mistakes: reciting too slowly, too fast, with the words not clear, and so forth.

Reciting with different rhythms is to give some idea, especially to the very new people, of the way to recite the mantra. Even if it's not possible for you to recite the mantra fast at the moment, the general idea is to make it go faster and faster.

ADDITIONAL OFFERINGS

> "The savior of us transmigratory beings abides
>   magnificently,
> Having achieved the five holy bodies and wisdoms,
> And with the compassion that benefits others,
> Manifests in whatever aspect subdues us:
> To you, I offer the five sets of five.
> May we transmigratory beings achieve the five
>   holy bodies and wisdoms.
> OM PANCH PANCH VIMALA PUNDZA MEKA AH HUM."

The "five sets of five" are the five medicines, five grains, five jewels, five scented smells and five essences.

So far I haven't found the detailed names of all these substances— I might find them later in a different text. They might be the ingredients in the Kriya Tantra or Highest Yoga Tantra pills that go into the vase water. Maybe the many substances in those pills are the five sets of five, but I'm not sure. I checked in one text, but I didn't find the names.

You can put the five grains, for example, in one container, and then offer it on the altar in front of Chenrezig. When you recite the verse, you offer one container of jewels, one container of perfumes, or scented smells, and so forth. I'm not sure about the five essences, but they might be milk, curd, butter, honey and sugar. You make offering of the five sets of five to Compassion Buddha.

In regard to counting five holy bodies, or kayas, there is the *Svabhavikakaya*, the ultimate nature of the omniscient mind, of Buddha's holy mind; the *Dharmakaya* (or *ye-she chö-ku*, in Tibetan), the transcendental wisdom of the omniscient mind; then the manifestations of this, the *Rupakaya*, which has two divisions: the *Sambhogakaya* (or *long-chö tsob-kyi-ku*, in Tibetan), the holy body of complete enjoyment, and the *Nirmanakaya*, the holy body of transformation. There are these four kayas.

In counting five kayas, it seems in one text one great Amdo lama counted the general term "chö-ku." Chö-ku, or Dharmakaya, which is sometimes translated as "truth body," has two divisions. *Ngo-wo nyi-ku*, or the holy body of nature, is the ultimate nature of the omniscient mind, which is totally free from temporary obscurations (as opposed to the ultimate nature of our mind, which is not free from the temporary obscurations); and *ye-she chö-ku*, or the wisdom body, is the transcendental wisdom of the omniscient mind itself.

When five kayas are counted, the general term "chö-ku" is mentioned. There are two types of omniscient mind: one that directly sees the ultimate nature, or absolute truth, of all phenomena and one that directly sees the conventional truth. So, maybe "ye-she chö-ku" refers to the omniscient mind that directly sees the ultimate nature of phenomena and the general term "chö-ku" refers to the omniscient mind that directly sees conventional truth phenomena. It could be that, but I'm not sure.

We also request the five wisdoms. We offer the five sets of five— five medicines, five grains, five jewels, five scented smells and five essences—then express the wish for what we want to achieve by making the offerings: "May we transmigratory beings achieve the five holy bodies and wisdoms."

There is also an offering mantra to offer these sets of five: OM PANCH PANCH VIMALA PUNDZA MEKA AH HUM. In Hindi "panch," as in "panch rupees," means five. At the end of each offering verse there is a mantra. When you offer the divine dress, the offering mantra is OM BENZA WA TRA YE AH HUM SOHA. When you offer ornaments, the mantra is OM BENZA ALAMKARA WA PUKANI AH HUM SOHA.

When you offer the vase, you pour out a drop of water, visualizing that you purify the karmas and delusions of the sentient beings of the six realms and that they then generate bodhicitta in their minds. This is as it is said in the prayer. Think that with the drop of water, all sentient beings purify all their karma and delusions and receive the moisture of bodhicitta. The offering mantra is OM BENZA KALASHA AH HUM. Then, when you offer these five sets of five, the mantra to recite is OM PANCH PANCH VIMALA PUNDZA MEKA AH HUM. In your mind, think that you offer to the merit field the various offerings that are set up on the altar.

It is also very good to offer the eight auspicious signs and the seven kings' reign. There is also a verse for this offering, but I haven't found it yet. I will have to look for it in another text. We can also set up these offerings on the altar. It would be good to put many offerings around the mandala. At the moment we have only the mandala, but maybe later we can have umbrellas and banners, the eight auspicious signs, the seven king's reign, the eight substances, and so forth. It would be very, very good to actually make the umbrellas and banners and put them on the altar around the mandala.

Each of the seven king's reign has its own signification, which is why they are given during initiations. It is an auspicious preparation to achieve each of the qualities of Buddha that they signify, which then enables you to do perfect work for sentient beings. It is the same here. Offering them to Chenrezig signifies achieving those qualities. And it is the same with the eight substances that we offer during long-life pujas. Each one has a different dedication for the achievement of the qualities that enable us to do perfect work for sentient beings. It's a very good practice, and we can do the same here.

I will look in another text for those offering verses, because they are very good to do. They are usually in self-initiation texts. Before the actual initiation, there are extensive offerings as a preliminary, which shows the importance of collecting merit. At the beginning you make extensive offerings to yourself clarified as the deity. If they didn't have a special purpose, there would be no reason for the extensive offerings of the seven royal emblems and so forth to always come during self-initiations.

In the mother tantra practices of Chakrasamvara and Vajrayogini, for example, there are the sixteen goddesses carrying various offerings. If it didn't have an important purpose, why would it be there? Because you have nothing to do and feel lonely, so you do it to fill in your time? It is not for just filling in time, like the many retired

71

people who have nothing to do in their life so they do something outside in the garden or go for a walk somewhere or fix this and that. They just spend their days in this way; otherwise, they are bored and don't know what to do with themselves. Making these offerings is not just to pass the time and fill in your day; there has to be a very important reason that offerings come in every practice. So, it would also be very good to have the extensive offerings here.

[Dinner bell rings in the background.] Oh, there is the bell offering. Okay, I will stop there....

9

Monday, December 25

AFTERNOON: THIRD MANI SESSION

CALLING THE LAMA FROM AFAR

While you are chanting, you can look at the meaning of the prayer in English. Or you can just read the prayer in English.

Visualize your root virtuous friend above your crown, with the recognition that in essence he is all the Buddhas. In order to guide you—to liberate you not only from the sufferings of the lower realms but also from the oceans of samsaric suffering and to bring you to enlightenment—all the Buddhas manifested in this human aspect. Think, "All the Buddhas manifested in this ordinary aspect, which shows faults and suffering, in accordance with my impure mistaken mind."

Calling the Guru from Afar is basically a meditation on the kindness of the guru. Each verse describes the extensive kindness of the guru, and you then make requests for the fulfillment of your wishes.

[Rinpoche chants the abbreviated *Calling the Lama from Afar* (p. 16).]

"May I not generate heresy for even one second toward the holy actions of the glorious guru, and with the devotion that sees whatever action is done as pure, may the blessing of the guru enter my heart."

You can then meditate on the guru entering the heart or melting into light. Those who have received a Highest Yoga Tantra initiation, such as Vajrasattva, can visualize that the guru absorbs into their heart in the same way; those who haven't received a great initiation can visualize that the guru melts into white light and is absorbed at the point between their eyebrows. Your own body, speech and mind are blessed into the vajra holy body, vajra holy speech and vajra holy mind.

It is said in the teachings that if you have received a Highest Yoga Tantra initiation, you can do the absorption through the crown into the heart. If you haven't received a Highest Yoga Tantra initiation, it is normally advised that you visualize the guru melting into light and absorbing at the point between your eyebrows. The same applies to the absorption of Guru Shakyamuni Buddha. After you have done the practice of refuge or the visualization of purifying negativities and receiving qualities, the refuge merit field in front of you melts into light and is absorbed at the point between your eyebrows. That is the normal instruction given in the teachings. When you are visualizing other deities, at the end, the deity returns to the natural abode or absorbs within your heart. If you haven't received a great initiation of Highest Yoga Tantra, you visualize that the deity melts into light then absorbs at the point between your eyebrows.

DEDICATIONS

"From now on, whatever actions I do—eating, walking, sitting, sleeping, working and so forth—and whatever life I experience—up or down; happy or unhappy; healthy or unhealthy; whether I have cancer (or any other disease) or I don't have cancer; whether my life is peaceful and harmonious or I have difficulties such as relationship problems; gain or loss; rich or poor; whether I receive praise from others or criticism; whether I am living or dying, or even born in a hell realm—the main purpose of my life is not just to be rich, healthy, peaceful, or to be free from cancer and other problems and live a long life. The meaning of my life is to be useful to others. Therefore, from now on, may whatever actions I do and whatever life I experience, including being born in the hell realms, be most beneficial for all sentient beings. May everything be most useful to all sentient beings. And what is the most useful thing? To cause all sentient beings to achieve full enlightenment in the quickest way possible—and that happens by my achieving enlightenment."

One particular dedication can be done in each session.

We can now do the next dedication. [The group reads "Just as the brave Manjushri...perform the noble bodhisattva's deeds." (p. 79) in *Combined Jorchö and Lama Chöpa Puja*.]

The particular emphasis of the first dedication is the meaning of life. It emphasizes that the purpose of life is not just to avoid the experience of difficulties in life, such as relationship problems, disharmony with others, obstacles to our Dharma practice and so forth. This dedication reminds us that the meaning of life is something else. For ordinary people success in life is defined in terms of how much money—how many billions of dollars—a person makes each year. This is what ordinary people mean by a good life; this is how they see the meaning of life. It has to be carefully explained that this is not sufficient, that it is wrong to regard only benefit in this life as meaningful. The meaning of life is something higher than that, something more special than that.

This dedication verse helps you to see that and also reminds you that whether you have a happy or unhappy life, whether you have problems or don't have problems, whether you are living or dying, and whether you are born in a pure realm or a hell realm, with compassion you should make everything useful for other sentient beings. Whether you experience success or failure, you make it useful through your compassion for others, through your thought to benefit others. By achieving enlightenment and then enlightening all sentient beings, you make everything most beneficial for all sentient beings. And that comes about through bodhicitta, through compassion for others.

You transform whatever happy and unhappy experiences happen to you, then utilize them in the path to enlightenment, so that all those experiences become the cause of happiness for all sentient beings. That is what this dedication is expressing. Through this dedication we are reminded of this essential practice. This way of understanding the meaning of life and of living our life brings the greatest happiness and fulfillment. It brings the greatest satisfaction in life and also the highest happiness of enlightenment.

ADDITIONAL OFFERINGS

I'm not going to go over the meaning of all the offerings; I think I explained them here some time ago when I gave a Chenrezig initiation. I'll just give you the verses for offering the eight substances, the seven signs of royalty and the eight auspicious signs. These verses can be recited right after the verse for offering the five sets of five. These offerings can also be set up around the deity's mandala.

From what I have mentioned during these past days, please do not think that I am saying that I am the deity. But if disciples from their side visualize or meditate in this way, they receive blessings and also enlightenment. They achieve all the realizations and full enlightenment, which is the cessation of all the faults of the mind and the completion of all the realizations. It has been mentioned because it has great benefit. All realizations come from the root, guru devotion.

"By offering the seven precious signs of royalty,
May I be victorious in the war with the four maras

And achieve the complete power to propagate the
Mahayana teaching,
In order to quickly lead transmigratory beings to eve
lasting supreme happiness."

This is like Guru Shakyamuni Buddha and His Holiness the Dalai Lama, who have total control over whatever way Dharma, sutra or tantra, needs to be taught to sentient beings.

This is a brief prayer to offer the seven signs of royalty. If you want to offer the seven individually and recite the benefit you receive from each one, you can do the verses from the Vajrayogini self-initiation. You offer each royal sign, then dedicate for sentient beings to achieve a specific benefit. When you want to make each offering more specifically and elaborately, you can use the verses for the extensive offerings from the Vajrayogini self-initiation, Heruka Lama Chöpa or the Yamantaka self-initiation. All the extensive self-initiation texts have the offering of each of the seven signs of royalty, along with its specific dedication for sentient beings. It is very nice to do.

If you want to do it in the briefest way, you can recite the verse above, which is just put together from here and there....

Next comes the offering of the eight auspicious signs and the eight substances. These are all offered to the guru during a long-life puja, with verses that mention what each one signifies and what qualities we disciples are requesting to achieve in order to be able to do extensive work for sentient beings and for the teaching of Buddha. By offering them, you receive the various benefits that are explained in the teachings. During a long-life puja, for each of the various offerings, it is said, "By offering this, this happens." It is the same here. By doing the practice of meditating on and offering each individual object, you achieve the benefits signified by each one. It's incredibly auspicious, and a preparation, due to dependent arising, to achieve those qualities.

I will translate as the Tibetan verses are written. There are two basic ways to translate, one way is to translate backwards and the other is to translate forwards, so that the verse follows the Tibetan line by line. Sometimes that is a little easier.

"Just by being touched, seen, heard or remembered,
These eight auspicious signs blessed by the
    Victorious Ones
Eliminate all inauspicious things and grant perfect
    sublimeness.
By this virtue, may I quickly and effortlessly achieve
The collections of the qualities of cessation and
    realizations and the works for others."

"The Victorious Ones" means the buddhas, and "perfect sublimeness" means all the qualities of buddha. "The works for others" actually refers to the four tantric activities of peace, increase, control and wrath, which one needs to do for sentient beings.

I will write down the names of these auspicious substances in Tibetan.

While reciting the verses, visualize all these offerings if you can. Visualize numberless of each of the seven royal emblems, so that the whole sky is filled with king's ministers, horses, wish-granting jewels, Dharmachakras, and the rest. Or at least offer what you have arranged on the altar.

Do the same thing with the eight auspicious signs and substances. Visualize the whole sky filled with the eight auspicious signs and substances, and offer them. And the dedication for what you want to achieve by offering these things is there, in brief, in the verse.

Rather than offering just drawings of each object, you can offer actual figures of the horse, the elephant, the conch shell and so forth. You can set up those elaborate offerings on the altar.

The seven signs of royalty are usually cast in silver or drawn on cards, but recently I started to actually buy figures of horses, elephants and so forth from shops. I did this for long-life pujas for both Geshe Sopa Rinpoche and Ribur Rinpoche, as it makes the offering more elaborate. I also did this with the eight substances, but one of them, *gi-wang*, is very difficult to find. This substance comes from human beings, cows and elephants and is used in medicines and also, I think, in incense. I don't know exactly what it is. It's not musk. It is usually said that if you take this substance from a human, you have to take it out while the person is asleep. Gi-wang also comes from cows and elephants. It is very rare and expensive, but the rest of the substances are easy to obtain.

I saw that when a long-life puja is offered at Namgyäl Dratsang, His Holiness the Dalai Lama's temple, the actual substances are offered rather than drawings of them. I think this is also done in the Sakya tradition. In most long-life pujas drawings of the substances are offered, but at Namgyäl Dratsang they offer the actual crab grass, mustard seed, sindura and so forth. I thought it would be better to offer the actual substances rather than just the drawings of them. During long-life pujas I now try to perform the offerings by using the actual substances.

So, I think that's all. Thank you very much.

10

Tuesday, December 26 (A)

Morning: *Combined Jorchö/Lama Chöpa Puja*

Chanting for Offering of Practice

I think the chanting you have been using for *ngö-sham yi-trul...*, the offering of practice [verse 33], can be done for *der-ni ring-du...* [*Final Lam-Rim Dedication Prayer*, p. 12 in *Dedication Prayers*], but it is better to use the previous chanting for *ngö-sham yi-trul....* For *der-ni ring-du...* this chanting is good, but I think even this chanting is not quite right—there has been some change in the last part of the line, I think.

The chanting of *ngö-sham yi-trul...* should be like that done in *Heruka Lama Chöpa*. This chanting is done with a higher voice. [Rinpoche chants the whole of verse 33.]

You should start with a high voice—even higher than I used. And I think this verse should be started straight with "ngö..." without the "w-o-o-o." I think it's better that way. Otherwise, the chanting sounds a little strange. [Rinpoche chants the whole verse again.]

When Lama Lhundrub chants this verse, he usually goes higher and higher, which is according to Pabongka's way of chanting, but somehow it doesn't happen with me. Lama Lhundrub practiced with the great Pabongka Dechen Nyingpo's attendant or umze. Usually the chanting is supposed to go higher and higher, near the end, but somehow it's not happening.... I think this is the style of chanting of Dagpo Shedrup Ling, the monastery of Pabongka's guru, which is on the way from Lhasa. Dagpo is the name of that area. I think it is the monastery of the Dagpo Rinpoche who now lives in France. Some monks from that monastery usually chant at the end of His Holiness the Dalai Lama's teachings. It's a little different from Pabongka's way of chanting. As I didn't have the good luck to actually hear the chanting from Pabongka himself, I'm not sure exactly what it is.

There's something that's not quite right near the end of your tune. Can you chant it again? Do the chanting of *der-ni ring-du...*, the dedication for the spread of the Dharma that comes at the end of the *Jorchö*.

[Ven. Tsapel sings *der-ni ring-du...kun-tu-yang....*]

That one is supposed to be the Pabongka chanting. There are different ways of chanting that. At the end of lam-rim teachings by His Holiness Trijang Rinpoche, they would normally chant that a little faster. [Rinpoche demonstrates a quicker chanting of *der ni ring du...jam päl yang kyi...*] I think I changed it a little bit! [Rinpoche chants *der ni ring du...nye je shog.*] This is how it is normally chanted at the end of lam-rim teachings, as far as I can remember.

This slow chanting that is used for *ngö sham yi trul...* is actually from Heruka Lama Chöpa, and Pabongka's attendant and those who learnt it from him commonly chant it this way. I didn't hear Pabongka himself chant, but I believe that it's Pabongka's way of chanting.

These days at the end of His Holiness the Dalai Lama's teachings, when monks from the Dagpo Shedrup Ling monastery are present, His Holiness asks them to chant this prayer according to the style of their monastery. It seems that His Holiness prefers it to be chanted in that way.

[Rinpoche chants the whole prayer.]

It's basically the same tune, but it goes up more sharply than that one and the last word is slightly longer. The end of the first line is longer and the next line goes a little higher at the end. It goes more smoothly, I think, but basically it's the same chanting.

Anyway, it might be something like that—I'm not sure!

So, enjoy your tea or whatever. Thank you.

11

Tuesday, December 26 (B)

MORNING: FIRST MANI SESSION

CHANTING FOR BRIEF MANDALA OFFERING

There are two mandalas in the nyung-nä sadhana, one offered here [p. 74] and the other offered later to the front generation. For this first mandala offering, it might be good to do the slow chanting of *sa-zhi pö-kyi*…, the chanting that is normally done when we request teachings. Maybe this chanting can be done in this session, and the usual chanting of *sa-zhi pö-kyi*… can be done for the mandala offering to the front generation. This chanting is that of the *en-sa nying-gyu*—usually translated as "Ensapa whispered lineage"—which is passed from ear to ear. I think that chanting was usually done in the early Kopan Courses then spread out to all the FPMT Centers from there.

You can also use this slow chanting for the auspicious prayer at the end.

[Ven. Tsapel starts to lead the slow chanting of *sa zhi pö kyi*….]

No, do the whole thing—do the whole construction!

[Ven. Tsapel leads the long mandala followed by the slow chanting of the brief mandala, inner mandala and auspicious prayer.]

THE *DHARANI* OF IMMACULATE MORALITY

[Rinpoche interrupts the recitation of OM AMOGHA SHILA SAMBHARA BHARA BHARA… (p. 87).]

The *Kangyur*, Buddha's teachings, explains the following benefits of reciting this mantra. I don't have the lineage of the oral transmission of the *Kangyur*, but I'll just explain the benefits that it mentions.

"I prostrate to all the Tathagatas of the three times. I prostrate to

Arya Avalokiteshvara (or in English, Lord Compassionate-eyed Looking One), who is the great hero bodhisattva with great compassion. If you keep the eight precepts of Reviving and Purifying (it's not talking here about the whole practice of nyung-nä, maintaining silence and so forth) and simply mentally or verbally recite this heart mantra twenty-one times, you will have great pure morality; you will complete the paramita of morality; many scented fragrances of morality will arise from your body; and you will become famous in the worlds of the ten directions. If you remember this mantra every day, your morality will always be completely pure. By abiding in the retreat (here it means, I think, taking the Eight Mahayana Precepts and being in silence) and simply reciting this mantra, any bhikshu who has degenerated his morality will completely purify his morality and be able to abide in many moralities." This is what Buddha explained in the *Kangyur*.

Also, my root guru, His Holiness Trijang Rinpoche, explained in a nyung-nä commentary that reciting this mantra purifies morality that has been degenerated and enables one to live in pure morality and to receive the perfect morality of all the buddhas.

My suggestion is that it would be very good for members of the Sangha to recite this mantra in their daily life. When you wake up in the morning, you should first rejoice that so far you have not died. Recollect impermanence and death very strongly, thinking that your death will happen today, at any moment. By first thinking of impermanence and death, you cut the eight worldly dharmas. Then generate a strong motivation of bodhicitta for your life. Give up the ego, the self-cherishing thought, and generate the thought to achieve enlightenment for sentient beings. From now on that becomes the motivation for all your activities. Think, "I'm going to do all my activities and all virtues for the benefit of sentient beings."

"Activities" refers to eating, walking, sitting, sleeping, working and so forth; "virtues" refers to the traditional practices of reciting sadhanas, doing prostrations and so forth. In other words, you do all these to benefit sentient beings. That is the idea. You dedicate in this way whatever activities and specific traditional practices you are going to do from now on.

After that, you can do prostrations to the Thirty-five Buddhas either alone or in a group in the gompa. After you finish the prostrations with the recitation of the names of the Thirty-five Buddhas and the accompanying prayer, even if you haven't done the ceremony for taking the Eight Mahayana Precepts, it might be useful to recite the OM AMOGHA SHILA… mantra at the end. Even if you have not taken the Eight Mahayana Precepts, you still have thirty-six vows, many more than the eight vows of the Eight Mahayana Precepts. Without talking about fully ordained monks or nuns, even a novice monk or nun has many more vows than the Eight Mahayana Precepts. I think that it would be very useful to recite this mantra, in the morning after doing prostrations, whether as a group or in your own house. As mentioned in the *Kangyur*, this mantra helps you to be able to keep your morality pure.

I just thought to mention that. Now my advertisement about the good qualities of this mantra is finished. So now, back to the news….

FOUR IMMEASURABLES

It would also be good to recite the four immeasurables [p. 87] in the other sessions, after refuge and bodhicitta. The reason the four immeasurables come before the actual meditation on emptiness and on the deity and mandala is that you collect merit like the limitless sky when you generate each immeasurable thought. According to this verse here, the first one is the immeasurable thought of loving kindness, the second is the immeasurable thought of compassion, the third is the immeasurable thought of joy and the fourth is the immeasurable thought of equanimity. With each one of them you collect limitless skies of merit.

We meditate on the four immeasurable thoughts before doing the rest of the practice because with each of them we collect extensive merit. To be born as a wheel-turning king, for example, you need to collect a lot of merit. To be born in the family of a wheel-turning king and become a wheel-turning king, with incredible wealth and power, you need to collect inconceivable merit. In a similar way, you need to collect extensive merit before meditating on the graduated generation stage, which prepares you to purify ordinary death, ordinary intermediate state and ordinary rebirth by meditating on the imagined three kayas: Dharmakaya, Sambhogakaya and Nirmanakaya. That is why in sadhanas meditating on the four immeasurable thoughts comes just before you engage in meditation on the three kayas.

Meditation on the four immeasurable thoughts is regarded as a very powerful means to collect merit. With each one you collect extensive merit, creating the cause of rebirth as a wheel-turning king and of enlightenment. As mentioned in *Liberation in the Palm of Your Hand*, you create the cause to be born innumerable times as a wheel-turning king.

Therefore, in the other sessions, when you abbreviate the practice, it would be very good to meditate on the four immeasurables after refuge and bodhicitta.

Now go back....

PRAISE

[Ven. Ailsa requests Rinpoche to demonstrate the chanting of the praise verse just before the mantra recitation (p. 102).]

I don't know how it will fit, but I'll try another tune—another fashion!

[Rinpoche chants *sang-gyä kün-gyi...chag-tsäl-lo.*]
I'll try one more time....
[Rinpoche chants the verse again.]
That was not very good....
[Rinpoche chants the verse again.]
I think I'll stop there.

DEDICATIONS

I have given a different dedication to be done at the end of each session. I have given you the one for the end of the *Guru Puja.* Here you can do the following dedication.

"Due to the merits of the three times collected by me and those collected by others, may any sentient being just by seeing me, touching me, remembering me, thinking about me, talking about me or even dreaming about me never ever be reborn in the lower realms from that time. May they immediately be liberated from all disease, spirit harms, negative karmas and defilements. May they achieve enlightenment as quickly as possible by actualizing the whole path to enlightenment, especially bodhicitta."

Before this dedication you should recite *ge-wa di-yi...* in English, adding "merely labeled" to the various elements. And after this dedication, you should do *jam-päl pa-wo...* then the prayer for the spread of Lama Tsong Khapa's teachings.

At the end of the next session, you can do the dedication about whatever action one does and whatever life one experiences to be most useful by becoming the cause for all sentient beings to achieve enlightenment as quickly as possible by oneself becoming enlightened.

At the end of another session, you can do the dedication I mentioned the other day, "Like the compassionate white lotus, may I become wish-fulfilling for all sentient beings." I'm not sure what the dedication for the final session is—I think the next dedication is all the thank-yous....

Morning: Second Mani Session

Praise

Maybe I'll try another chanting of the *Praise to Compassion Buddha* [p. 102].

[Rinpoche chants *sang-gyä kun-gyi…chag-tsäl-lo.*]

So, if that could be done slower—as slowly as possible.

Motivation for mantra recitation

This is another way to generate a motivation of bodhicitta before reciting the mantra, to make the recitation of mantra and the meditation on Compassion Buddha become not only Dharma but most beneficial not only for you but for every single hell being, hungry ghost, animal, human being, asura, sura and intermediate state being. Each realm has numberless beings. In the human realm there are numberless human beings. We can understand that there are numberless beings in the animal realm. Even in regard to one type of insect, ants, there are numberless ants. In the same way, there are many other different types of animals the number of which is uncountable. This is without mentioning the sentient beings in the other realms.

All these beings, who are the source of all your own past, present and future happiness, are continuously suffering; totally overwhelmed by delusions and karma, they do not have any freedom at all.

Even though there are numberless buddhas and bodhisattvas working for sentient beings, there are many sentient beings—people, and even animals—who received help only through meeting you. They had some problem they couldn't resolve until they met you and you were able to help them. Or they didn't meet Dharma until they met you. You have had many such experiences of sentient beings being dependent upon your help.

There are numberless beings with whom you have a karmic connection and who depend upon you. Their being free from suffering, from samsara, and their achieving liberation and enlightenment depend on you, on your help. You can understand from your experiences in this life of the many beings who depend on your help that there are numberless other beings who depend on your help to free them from samsara; they depend on you to meet, understand and practice Dharma and to achieve enlightenment.

Now think, "If I had generated bodhicitta much earlier, this one hell being who is dependent on me wouldn't have to experience this unimaginable, unbearable suffering, the heaviest suffering in samsara." One tiny spark of the fire of the hot hells is seven times hotter than the fire at the end of the world, which can melt rocky mountains and concrete. And the fire at the end of the world is sixty or seventy times hotter than the fire energy of our present human world.

"For one hell being to be suffering now in the hell realm even for one second is like eons—it is unbearable. If I had generated bodhicitta much earlier, that hell being would already have been enlightened. Now we are talking about just one hell being, but there are numberless other hell beings who could have already been enlightened by me, so that they wouldn't now have to suffer. They have been suffering up to now because I have been following the self-cherishing thought, the ego. Therefore, even when I think of this one hell being who is experiencing unimaginable suffering, it becomes urgent that I generate bodhicitta without even a second's delay. Now there are numberless hell beings; therefore, I need to generate bodhicitta without the delay of even a second. Because there are numberless hell beings who are suffering, the need for me to generate bodhicitta is much more urgent.

"If I had generated bodhicitta much earlier, this one preta being, who is so precious and kind and from whom I receive all my past, present and future happiness would have already been enlightened. But because I followed self-cherishing thought, this one preta being has been suffering so much, experiencing all the unbearable sufferings of heat, cold, exhaustion, hunger and thirst, outer obscurations, food obscurations and inner obscurations. And there are numberless preta beings. If I had generated bodhicitta earlier, all these number-less preta beings would already have been enlightened. Because I didn't generate bodhicitta, they have been suffering up to now. Therefore, it is urgent: I *must* generate bodhicitta without the delay of even a second, not just for this one hungry ghost but for the numberless hungry ghosts.

"If I had generated bodhicitta much earlier, this one animal who has been suffering so much up to now—being extremely foolish, experiencing hunger and thirst, heat and cold, being tortured, used for food—would already have been enlightened a long time ago. There are numberless animals, and they would all have already been enlightened if I had generated bodhicitta much earlier. It is because I didn't generate bodhicitta but followed the ego that they have been suffering up to now. Therefore, the need for me to generate bod-hicitta, to change my mind, is unbelievably urgent, not only for this one animal but for the numberless animals who have been experi-encing so much suffering.

"And it is the same with the human beings. If I had generated bodhicitta, if I had changed my mind, a long time ago, this one human being, who is constantly suffering, would already have been enlightened. Instead they are experiencing the suffering of pain; if not that, the suffering of change; and if not that, pervasive compounding suffering, by having these aggregates, this samsara, the nature of which is suffering. These aggregates are caused by karma and delusions and contaminated by the seed of disturbing thoughts, so this person constantly, without the break of even one second, experiences pervasive compounding suffering. In this way, this human being is totally overwhelmed by delusion and karma, living in a total hallucination, with piles of wrong concepts, and suffering in that way. If I had generated bodhicitta earlier, this most precious and kind human being who has been suffering up to now and who is the source of all my own past, present and future happiness, would already have been enlightened and not have to suffer. And there are numberless human beings. Because I did not change my mind but followed the ego, not only this one human being but numberless human beings have been suffering during time without beginning up to now. Therefore, without the delay of even a second, I must change my mind into bodhicitta, into cherishing others.

"It is similar with the suras. If I had generated bodhicitta much earlier, this one sura being who has been suffering so much would have been enlightened a long time ago. The sufferings of the suras are similar to those I mentioned for human beings. Suras are also totally distracted by objects of desire; they cling to and are distracted by sense pleasures. No matter how many eons they live, their life is totally overwhelmed by desire. In this way, they suffer so much and are constantly creating the cause of suffering, the cause to again be reborn in the lower realms. Their having great enjoyments is just temporary. How wonderful it would have been if this one sura being could have been enlightened a long time ago. And there are numberless sura beings who would have been enlightened a long time ago. How fantastic if that could have happened. Because I didn't change my mind, but instead followed only the ego, not only this one being but numberless sura beings have been suffering up to now. And it is similar with the asuras.

"My kind mother sentient beings have been suffering from time without beginning; they have never had a break for even one second from the suffering of samsara, from pervasive compounding suffering. Therefore, without delay, I *must* generate bodhicitta. Generating bodhicitta depends on receiving the blessing of the special deity of compassion. Trying to develop bodhicitta just by remembering the words of the teachings is not enough. Even meditation alone is not enough. I need to receive the blessings of the special deity of compassion. For that reason, I need to meditate on Compassion Buddha and to recite the mantra that persuades Compassion Buddha's holy mind. I need to recite the mantra that brings me closer to the deity of compassion, that causes me to receive the blessings of the deity of compassion. Therefore, I'm going to do the meditation-recitation of Compassion Buddha."

Maybe there's time now to recite one mantra—just one!

You can recite the long mantra once, then OM MANI PADME HUM....

FOOD OFFERING

"The purpose of my life is to free all sentient beings from all their sufferings and bring them to full enlightenment. Therefore, I must achieve enlightenment; therefore, I'm going to practice the yoga of eating, making charity to all sentient beings." There are also sentient beings living inside your body and, through the connection made by offering charity to them at this time, you will be able to bring them to enlightenment by revealing Dharma to them when they become human beings. "I'm also going to make food offering to the guru, Buddha, Dharma and Sangha. I'm going to do the practice of the yoga of eating, making charity to all sentient beings and making food offering to the guru, Buddha, Dharma and Sangha."

All the food in the kitchen is purified in emptiness, as it *is* empty from its own side. While it is empty, the wisdom understanding emptiness manifests as the syllable BHRUM, which transforms into extensive jeweled containers, inside of which the syllable OM, which signifies the Buddha's holy body, holy speech and holy mind, melts into light and becomes oceans of uncontaminated nectar.

The numberless Buddhas receive numberless food nectar offerings. The *Guru Puja* merit field receives numberless food nectar offerings. If you are not familiar with the *Guru Puja* merit field, you can think of Shakyamuni Buddha. For the visualization during this retreat, the principal figure is Guru Compassion Buddha. You can also visualize all the direct and indirect lineage lamas, deities, Buddhas—including the buddhas of the fortunate eon, the Thirty-five Buddhas, the Medicine Buddhas and so forth—bodhisattvas, dakas and dakinis, and Dharma protectors.

Before that, we should do the blessing.

OM AH HUM (3x)

Offer numberless food nectar to them, by meditating that in essence they are your root virtuous friend. The nectar generates infinite bliss within them. Prostrate with your two palms together to all of them.

Offer numberless food nectar to all the Buddha, Dharma and Sangha of the ten directions, by meditating that in essence they are your root virtuous friend. The nectar generates infinite bliss within them. Prostrate with your two palms together to all the Buddha, Dharma and Sangha of the ten directions.

Offer numberless food nectar to all the statues, stupas, scriptures and thangkas in all the universes in the ten directions. By making the offering, you generate infinite bliss within them. Prostrate with your two palms together to all of them.

Now make charity of numberless nectar offerings to every single hell being, every single hungry ghost, every single animal being, every single human being, every single asura being, every single sura being, every single intermediate state being. They all fully enjoy the nectar; they are all liberated from all their suffering and its causes and become enlightened in the aspect of Compassion Buddha.

We collected limitless skies of merit, of good karma—or good luck—by having generated a motivation of bodhicitta. During the blessing, we collected limitless skies of merit by having made offering to all the buddhas of the ten directions—or maybe we didn't do that! We collected limitless skies of merit by having made numberless food nectar offerings to Guru Chenrezig and all the rest of the merit field. By offering to all the Buddha, Dharma and Sangha of the ten directions, we collected limitless skies of merit. By offering to all the statues, stupas, scriptures and thangkas in the ten directions, we collected four times limitless skies of merit. Then, by having made charity to all sentient beings, we collected limitless skies of merit.

With each offering we created numberless causes of enlightenment, numberless causes of liberation from samsara, numberless causes to receive a good rebirth. From each offering we receive a good rebirth for hundreds or thousands of lifetimes.

And just by prostrating with our hands together, we collected numberless times eight benefits, the last of which is liberation from samsara and full enlightenment.

"Due to all these merits that we have collected now, as well as our past and future merits and the merits of the three times collected by others, may I, the members of my family, all the students and benefactors of the FPMT and all the rest of the sentient beings never be separated from the guru-Triple Gem, always collect merit by making offerings to the guru-Triple Gem and receive the blessings of the guru-Triple Gem, which are all the realizations from guru devotion up to enlightenment, especially bodhicitta and clear light. May these realizations be actualized within my own mind and in the minds of all other sentient beings without the delay of even a second.

"Due to all the past, present and future merits collected by me and the merits of the three times collected by others (which exist, but do not exist from their own side), may the I (which exists, but does not exist from its own side, which is empty) achieve Compassion Buddha's enlightenment (which exists, but doesn't exist from its own side, which is empty) and lead all sentient beings (who exist, but do not exist from their own side, who are totally empty) to that enlightenment (which exists, but doesn't exist from its own side, which is totally empty) by myself *alone* (who exists, but doesn't exist from my own side, who is totally empty)."

la ma sang gyä la ma chö
de zhin la ma ge dün te
kün gyi je po la ma te
la ma nam la chö par bül

So, thank you very much. Enjoy the nectar!

13

Tuesday, December 26 (C)

EVENING: FINAL MANI SESSION

HAIR-CUTTING CEREMONY

Good afternoon—or good evening!

I think that before reciting *The King of Prayers*, Samantabhadra's prayer, we will do the cutting of the crown hair for two people. This is not an actual ordination, but it is a preparation that directs the life toward taking the ordination of renunciation, which refers to renouncing the householder's life and the worldly life. It also leads to the *getsul* ordination, which means taking thirty-six vows, which is the preliminary to the full ordination of a *gelong*, or *bhikshu*. Cutting the crown hair is a preparation for that.

[Rinpoche chants Homage to Shakyamuni Buddha and other prayers in Tibetan.]

"The ordination of body, which means abstaining from the negative karmas of the body, is good; the ordination of the speech is good; the ordination of the mind is good. The whole ordination, which means abstaining from all the negative karmas of body, speech and mind, is good. The bhikshu who abstains from all of them and lives in all the vows will be liberated from all suffering. One who protects the speech, the mind and the body from non-virtuous activities and who lives purely in the three paths of action will achieve the path that is taught by the sage (which means by Buddha). Due to these merits, by achieving the enlightenment of the omniscient one, may I subdue the shortcomings of the enemy and may I liberate others."

It is saying, "Due to these merits, may I achieve the state of omniscient mind and subdue the shortcomings of the enemy and liberate the transmigratory beings from the oceans of samsara, from the turmoil of the waves of old age, sickness and death."

Kneel down with your hands like this. Now some of their nose will be cut off—I'm joking!

When I ask, "Are you happy to have your crown hair cut?" you say, "Yes."

Are you happy to have your crown hair cut? [Freeman: Yes.] [Rinpoche recites a short prayer in Tibetan.]

Did you have a Dharma name before? [Freeman: No.] Thubten Gyaltsen is your name.

When I ask the question, "Are you happy to have your crown hair cut?" you have to say, "Yes."

Are you happy to have your crown hair cut? [John: Yes.] [Rinpoche recites a short prayer in Tibetan.] You have a Dharma name from before? [John: Yes.] Unless you want to make it longer— I'm joking.

The basic reason for cutting the crown hair is that the hair is a part of the body that is generally a big object of attachment. This happened when Buddha was in India, and according to Indian culture, even if Hindus shave the rest of their head, they still keep one long lock of hair, and I think that they cling very much to that lock of hair. Shaving the head means to renounce that. I think nowadays shaving the head has become fashionable. Even in the West, you see many people now with shaved heads, especially singers and musicians. Previously, however, a shaved head was regarded as very ugly.

Cutting the crown hair is to show renunciation, to free the mind from attachment. It is to show detachment from the lay marks, or signs, of long hair and nails. It is all to show detachment from samsara and samsaric perfections, by seeing that samsara is suffering in nature.

It shows that the person is looking for liberation, and the basic path to liberation is the three higher trainings. What actually cuts the delusions is great insight, or wisdom. It is, of course, the wisdom that directly perceives emptiness that directly ceases the delusions; however, in order to achieve that, you need to achieve great insight, which is the wisdom realizing emptiness unified with the realization of calm abiding (*shamatha* in Sanskrit or *shiné* in Tibetan). By doing analysis and equipoise meditation, you derive the extremely refined bliss of body and mind, which characterizes the experience of great insight.

The realization of great insight depends on having first achieved calm abiding, and that depends on living in pure morality. The foundation is living in pure morality. Wisdom cuts the delusions and calm abiding controls the delusions, but both are based on living in morality, on the body and speech abstaining from negative karma. Morality is living in the vows to abstain from the negative actions of body and speech.

The basic motivation for taking the vows is detachment from samsara and samsaric perfections and the wish for liberation. That is why the dress is also changed. I think Christians have something similar; they also give up the lay signs of lay dress, long hair and long nails. Other traditions may have the same thing, but here the reason is much deeper. In the other religions there is no talk of renouncing samsara and so forth. Renouncing the suffering of pain may be mentioned in other religions, but the suffering of change is not usually mentioned, and even if it is mentioned, pervasive compounding suffering is not mentioned. Real liberation, which is cessation of pervasive compounding suffering, is not mentioned in other religions.

The whole external change has to do with cutting attachment

and keeping the mind peaceful, happy and satisfied. I think it is done mainly to create the conditions for a calm, peaceful mind, a mind that is free of attachment.

For the past two or three years, I have been taking teachings from Geshe Sopa Rinpoche in Wisconsin. The first year was on the great insight section of the lam-rim. The second year was on Lama Tsong Khapa's important text *The Good Explanation of the Interpretive and Definitive Meaning*. Geshe-la taught it over two years and finished it this year.

In the first or second year, Brandon, Roger [Kunsang]'s nephew, was there; he was a monk then, but now he is no longer a monk. And Roger [Munro] and Paula, who had become monk and nun, were also there. When we went shopping together, people in the street were very interested in us and often asked questions. I think they liked the robes. They were also very curious and would ask, "What are you?" or "What does this mean?" It seems that sometimes they would be given a very simple explanation that didn't give them a broad understanding.

Roger and Paula both did three-year retreats at Milarepa Center in Vermont; he did Heruka Body Mandala retreat and she did Vajrayogini retreat. They are both now doing a three-year Yamantaka retreat on the advice of Ribur Rinpoche. They started this year. Roger is doing his retreat at Calm Abiding Land, a very isolated place. I waited many years to find such a place where calm abiding could be achieved. It is very isolated and extremely quiet. When I first went there, I didn't hear even any insect noises. Maybe from time to time there is a little noise from airplanes. Roger is now doing retreat there, and Paula is doing retreat at Vajrapani Institute.

Anyway, during one mealtime, when we were all sitting together, I asked each monk and nun how they explained when somebody asked them what they were. Each person gave his or her own ideas, and then I gave a few suggestions about what we should explain to people. It was a few lines, though I don't remember them now, that made it very easy to explain when people asked questions and also gave them a broad view, rather than a narrow understanding. I think it's important because people are always asking such questions.

There is now an auspicious prayer. I'll explain the meaning so that everybody can think about it as I recite the prayer.

"May the body be auspicious with the three types of robes. May the speech be auspicious with the three baskets of teachings. May the mind be auspicious with the three higher trainings. And may they be beautified by the ornaments of the three higher trainings."

[Rinpoche recites the prayer in Tibetan.]

And everybody please dedicate for Thubten Gyaltsen and Losang Khedrub to be able to live in pure morality—not only in this life but in all their lifetimes—to complete the paramita of morality and to complete their life in celibacy. Pray for them in this way.

[Prayer in Tibetan.]

Dedicate to actualize bodhicitta. [*jang-chub sem-chog....*]

Dedicate to actualize wisdom. [*tong-ye ta-wai rinpoche....*]

Like Lama Tsong Khapa, may they be able to bring benefit as extensive as the sky to all sentient beings in all their lifetimes, by achieving the same qualities within them as Lama Tsong Khapa.

BENEFITS OF CHENREZIG PRACTICE

Reciting the Compassion Buddha's mantra can purify any heavy negative karma that one has collected. One great pandit, a fully ordained monk, broke all four root vows. With much regret, he then recited Compassion Buddha's mantra. After his death, when he was in front of Yama because of his heavy negative karma,

Chenrezig, Hayagriva and many other deities immediately protected him and he went to a pure land.

One lama told the family who were his neighbors, "I'm going to Compassion Buddha's pure land." The family then said, "If you're going to the pure land, please take us with you!" When the lama then asked Compassion Buddha about this (I guess he was able to see Compassion Buddha), Compassion Buddha said, "No, they cannot go, because they have eaten from wrong livelihood. They have eaten food with the money from selling the text, the *Prajnaparamita in 8,000 Stanzas*. This has heavily obscured their minds, so they cannot go to the pure land." When the lama then asked what they could do, Compassion Buddha replied, "Recite my mantra." So, with much regret, they then recited the manta, purified their heavy negative karma and went to the pure land.

There are many such stories. Reciting this mantra can purify any heavy negative karma.

Even by reciting OM MANI PADME HUM one time, you collect the same merit as having made offering to an inconceivable number of buddhas. You will see Buddha's face at the time of your death; and at the end of this life you will be born in whichever pure land of Buddha you wish.

By doing one prostration to Compassion Buddha and reciting the name of the Compassion Buddha even once, you collect the same amount of merit as having offered service to Buddhas equal in number to sixty-two times the number of sand grains of the Ganges River. That is an unbelievable amount of merit, and you collect the same amount of merit just by doing one prostration to Compassion Buddha and mentioning the name "Avalokiteshvara" just once.

Therefore, if one does—or even attempts to do—a nyung-nä correctly and with single-pointed devotion with recitation of the

Compassion Buddha's mantra, prostrations and offerings, there is no doubt that one's very heavy negative karmas are purified and one collects inconceivable merit.

It also says, "Any person who does the nearing retreat of nyung-nä well becomes meaningful to behold, just like Compassion Buddha. Anybody who touches that person or is touched by that person, any being who sees that person (even ants, mosquitoes or fleas—maybe there are no fleas here), and anybody who receives that person's breath purifies the negative karma that causes them to be born in the lower realms. When the breath of a person who has done a nyung-nä retreat well mixes with the air and that air then touches another sentient being, it purifies the negative karma that causes them to be reborn in the lower realms. If that person goes to the top of a mountain, any sentient being who sees them does not get reborn in the lower realms." It is similar when you go anywhere where there are a lot of people: to a supermarket, a restaurant or a train station like Old Delhi Train Station. You become meaningful for all the people who see you; they won't be reborn in the lower realms.

Here in the text it says "on top of a mountain," because you are high up and many people can see you. But it is the same in the street, at the beach, in a supermarket or restaurant and also in teachings, where many people can see you. All those hundreds or thousands of people, however many see you, don't go to the lower realms, because seeing you purifies the negative karma that causes them to be reborn in the lower realms. It is unbelievable! It becomes so meaningful. If you do healing or massage other people, it becomes meaningful for whomever you touch. Giving blessings, doing massage, healing, even shaking hands or touching people or animals becomes meaningful to those beings. It purifies their mind, and they won't be reborn in the lower realms.

When such a person swims in water or crosses water, any sentient being, animal or human, who drinks or is touched by the water that has touched that person won't get born in the lower realms.

Here these benefits are mentioned in relation to nyung-nä practice, but another text also mentions that if you recite just ten malas of OM MANI PADME HUM each day, if you go swimming, the water that touches your body will get blessed, and all the billions of sentient beings in the ocean, river or lake in which you have swum will be purified. Anybody who drinks that water or is touched by it won't be reborn in the lower realms. I think I have mentioned this many times during Compassion Buddha initiations, as many of you might remember.

Also, if you recite ten malas of OM MANI PADME HUM every day, your children, your grandchildren, their children, their children, their children, their children and their children—that is, seven generations—won't be reborn in the lower realms. This shows that it's very important for those who have many children or who are planning to have many children to recite ten malas of OM MANI PADME HUM each day. Up to seven generations are affected, because your blood is blessed by the power of mantra and also by visualizing yourself as Compassion Buddha. Each time you visualize yourself as Compassion Buddha, you are blessing your body, and each time you visualize the place as a mandala, you are blessing the place. Just as you transform this gompa into the Chenrezig mandala each time you do the sadhana, each time you do a sadhana that has a mandala in your own house or room, you are blessing that place. Each time you purify the place in emptiness, then visualize the mandala and the appearance of the deity's holy body, you are blessing, or consecrating, your house. You should know that you are blessing the place, as well as your own body. So, the blessing of your body affects the consciousness of your children. The blessing, or positive energy, that your body carries affects the minds of your children. This is the logical explanation of why your children, when they die, will die with a virtuous thought and not be reborn in the lower realms.

And when a person who recites ten malas of OM MANI PADME HUM each day dies, if he or she is cremated, the smoke from the fire will purify the negative karma of any sentient being who smells or is touched by it, so that being will not be reborn in the lower realms. Since even the shadow of such a person purifies the negative karma of any person, animal or insect that it touches, there is no doubt that anybody who touches that person purifies their negative karma and is liberated from the lower realms. They are also able to go to a pure land, such as the Amitabha pure land.

Because of the power of mantra, when there is danger of attack from a vicious animal or poisonous snake, one won't be harmed if one recites this mantra. Reciting this mantra stops the danger of being attacked in wars or by enemies and of being robbed. By relying upon the Compassion Buddha's mantra, you are freed from the danger of being punished by a king or in a court case. You are also not harmed by poisons. Also, a pregnant woman who does the practice of Compassion Buddha or simply recites Compassion Buddha's mantra, will be able to give birth comfortably, without severe pain. Also, one will be protected from the harm of black magic and evil mantras.

If intense desire or another strong delusion arises, chanting this mantra will naturally pacify it. Also, reciting the mantra and then blowing or spitting on sites of inflammation or infection can heal various sicknesses.

These are just some of basic benefits of reciting this mantra and of doing nyung-näs.

I want to mention here that for the nearing retreat, one recites 600,000 OM MANI PADME HUMs and then does a fire puja at the end. If you recite a long mantra—more than thirty or thirty-five syllables, I think—you can do a fire puja after reciting 10,000 mantras. His Holiness Serkong Tsenshab Rinpoche used to say that one could do a fire puja if one recited the long Chenrezig mantra 40,000 times. This probably means OM DHARA DHARA DHIRI DHIRI.... I don't know how many syllables it has. But if a mantra has more than thirty-five syllables, reciting 10,000 of them is a complete retreat, and you can then do a fire puja.

Because here you are doing the actual sadhana in each session, you can do a fire puja at the end if you have recited 600,000 OM MANI PADME HUMs. Since we are reciting many millions of mantras, it would be very good to do a fire puja to complete the retreat. Because you visualize yourself as Compassion Buddha, you are performing an actual retreat of Compassion Buddha, which means that you can do a fire puja at the end. In this way you can then perform consecrations, self-initiations, initiations and other activities. Of course, after having done many millions of mantras, it is very good to do a fire puja, as one has incidentally accomplished the retreat of Compassion Buddha.

I mentioned the other day that if you recite six or seven million OM MANI PADME HUMs, your saliva has much power to heal. You can then heal any kind of sickness. You can bless water or blow on butter or [hand] cream, which can be applied to the site of pain, or the water can be drunk for internal sicknesses. You can heal even by blowing on someone. You can not only heal sicknesses but also perform various activities to help other sentient beings by stopping their problems. You can perform the activities of peace, increase, control and wrath. You can also easily make or stop rain. All these various activities to benefit others happen incidentally. They are not main goal. The main goal is to achieve enlightenment and then liberate sentient beings from their suffering and bring them to enlightenment, but these other benefits, such as the ability to heal, happen incidentally.

THE LONG CHENREZIG MANTRA

After a little explanation, I will give the oral transmission of the very long Chenrezig mantra. Chinese communities recite this very long mantra for many hours, but it is not generally known among Tibetans. Of course, high lamas know about it, but not the common Tibetan people. You don't normally hear about this mantra, but it is commonly recited in the Chinese community. Some Chinese recite it very correctly, with the actual Sanskrit pronunciation, but many recite it in a broken way, like Tibetans reciting Sanskrit mantras where you can't tell what they are reciting. They are actually reciting the long Compassion Buddha mantra, but because the words are so distorted, you can't recognize it. They do still gain benefit, however, because they have so much devotion. The attainment from mantra recitation comes from devotion, not from how closely the words approximate the Sanskrit pronunciation.

I think I may have given this oral transmission in the past, but I don't remember clearly.

If you recite this long mantra seven times in one night, you purify eight hundred million eons of negative karma. It also brings much benefit to the spirits and other beings that are around. I thought to give the oral transmission of this mantra, which I received from Kirti Tsenshab Rinpoche. Again, this has unbelievable skies of benefit.

BENEFITS OF OFFERINGS

The ultimate benefit of making the offerings (*argham, padyam, pushpe, dhupe, aloke, gandhe, naividya* and *shapta*) and offering the tormas at the end of the session is, of course, liberation from samsara and enlightenment. But in the meantime, while you are in samsara, the temporary benefits are that you have a healthy, well-developed body and that you don't experience poverty.

The specific benefit of offering water is that your mental continuum becomes very calm and peaceful. You immediately feel this after you have offered water—not just filled up bowls with water, but really offered the water. His Holiness Song Rinpoche said in one Dharma Celebration that unless you do the meditation that accompanies the water offering, there is little purpose in just filling bowls with water, emptying them out and filling them again. I remember Rinpoche mentioning this, but I don't remember the actual meditation that Rinpoche explained.

This is a little like the way my mother used to listen to teachings from Trulshig Rinpoche or Trulshig Rinpoche's guru. She didn't understand when the lama explained the actual teaching about chakras, winds, drops and so forth; she would just keep on saying OM MANI PADME HUM, OM MANI PADME HUM, OM MANI PADME HUM, OM MANI PADME HUM. She didn't bother trying to understand the actual teachings. But if the lama said, "When you recite one mantra, don't move two beads," she understood perfectly. She would not only understand these kinds of things but always remember them, as well. Because of that, when she recited mantras, she didn't recite them very fast. She would recite OM MANI PADME HUM quite slowly, about the same speed as I was reciting the slightly quicker one. She did not always recite the same mantra, but the recitation was never fast.

In the breaks between the sessions of teaching, the lama would give advice, such as how you should behave when you go to see your guru: that you should sit in a respectful, humble manner with your two hands clasped together. She would understand these kinds of things very well and always remember them. Whenever she saw other lamas or came to sit in my room, she would always sit with her hands like this. [Rinpoche places his hands one on top of the other.] One of my uncles—I have many uncles, but this is the youngest one—also does this. She understood these things, but when the lama returned to the text or to talking about the path, she wouldn't bother to try to understand; she would just concentrate on OM MANI PADME HUM.

In any case, she couldn't understand what was being said, but she didn't waste her time because she chanted OM MANI PADME HUM during the teaching.

Offering water makes the mental continuum calm and clear, and you can feel this right after offering water. Unfortunately I don't offer water bowls every day; other people offer my water bowls for me. But on the rare occasions that I do offer them, I have noticed that right after offering the water you feel an effect, your mind feels somehow clear and peaceful. I'm sure that those of you who have been doing many water offerings have much experience of this. Offering water brings a calm, clear mind and increases the qualities, or realizations, within your mental continuum.

This is just a brief explanation of the very essence of the benefit. I'm not going to go into the much more extensive explanation of the benefits that is given in the sutra teachings.

Offering light increases wisdom—not just general wisdom, but Dharma wisdom. This is not the kind of wisdom that knows how many people in Australia have short hair and how many have long hair. It means the Dharma wisdom that knows what is right and to be practiced and what is wrong and to be abandoned. Dharma wisdom helps us to achieve happiness, especially liberation from samsara, from all suffering and its causes, and full enlightenment; with Dharma wisdom, we are able to realize the four noble truths and thus achieve liberation from samsara. So, offering light develops Dharma wisdom.

It is very important to offer as many lights as possible in everyday life. As explained in the sutra teachings, offerings have ten general benefits, and each offering also has its own specific benefits. Any offering to Buddha will always be a cause of enlightenment and of liberation from samsara, as well as other general benefits such as achieving a good rebirth in the next life. These benefits are common to any offering you make to Buddha.

Offering thousands of candles, of course, takes time and also requires a lot of space. If you don't have much space in your house, you can offer many small electric lights. You can buy many different sizes of bulbs, some small, some a little larger. It is then very easy to offer thousands of lights in your house, and it doesn't cost much. There are other things we use for enjoyment in our everyday life that cost much more than light offerings. Every day we spend so much more money than it would cost to make many thousands of light offerings with Christmas lights. We spend so much money in other ways that do not become the causes of enlightenment and liberation from samsara, or even a good rebirth in our next life.

Light offerings also help us to achieve clairvoyance, because light dispels darkness. Since we make the offering to holy objects, it dispels the darkness there around them. If you have an altar in your house, it is good to always have a light offering on it, even while you are sleeping. It's good not to leave the altar in darkness, but to offer light there all the time. Your mind is dark, the altar is dark, your life is also dark—everything is dark. It should not be like that. When you do not have a good heart and do not practice Dharma, your life is dark, filled with guilt or depression; there's no light in your life.

Without thinking of the guru but just of Buddha, the merit of every single offering to Buddha is inconceivable. Just offering one tiny stick of incense or one flower to a statue, painting or scripture of Buddha or by thinking of Buddha has inconceivable merit, even if the motivation is one of worldly concern, attachment clinging to this life, or of anger. Even if the motivation is totally non-virtuous and even if the offering is tiny (one small flower, one grain of rice or one small stick of incense), as long as the offering is made to a holy object, such as a statue or picture of Buddha, the benefit is unimaginable. As mentioned in the prayer and in the teachings, "Buddha has inconceivable qualities, Dharma has inconceivable qualities, Sangha has inconceivable qualities, and devotion to them also has inconceivable ripening aspect results." It results in inconceivable happiness—even the happiness is inconceivable—which you can experience for hundreds or thousands of lifetimes and in liberation from samsara and enlightenment.

It is good to know that whenever we make offering to a statue or a picture of Buddha or simply think of Buddha and offer, it immediately becomes the cause for us to achieve enlightenment. Now, you have to think in the following way. How can you achieve enlightenment without actualizing its cause, the graduated path to enlightenment? There is no way. Every single offering—even a tiny stick of incense, a tiny amount of rice or a flower—that you offer to a statue or a picture of Buddha immediately becomes a cause of enlightenment. It means it becomes a cause to achieve all the lam-rim meditations. It becomes a cause to realize guru devotion, renunciation of this life, renunciation of samsara, perfect human rebirth (its usefulness, the difficulty of achieving it again), impermanence and death, the suffering of the lower realms, and refuge and karma. It becomes a cause to realize how samsara is suffering in nature, the four noble truths (true suffering, true cause of suffering, cessation of suffering and true path) and the five paths to liberation. We are creating the cause to achieve all those realizations. There is so much to study about the five paths and the ten bhumis, as explained in *Abhisamayalankara*. And every single offering we make to Buddha becomes a cause to achieve all of them. On top of that comes the tantric path: the lower tantras, with the yoga having sign and the yoga not having sign, and Highest Yoga Tantra, with the generation and completion stages. This offering becomes a cause to achieve all those paths.

It is not that the offering becomes a cause to achieve enlightenment but does not become a cause of these realizations. Becoming a cause of enlightenment means that it becomes a cause to achieve every single realization of the path to enlightenment.

You can now see that every single holy object—every tsa-tsa, every picture of Buddha, whether big or tiny—is so precious. It is the real wish-fulfilling gem. These holy objects are the source of our happiness. From them we can achieve all the happiness up to enlightenment. All the good things that we can achieve and all the happiness that we can bring to all the numberless sentient beings come in dependence upon the power of these holy objects. Even a tiny picture of Buddha—and in a photo of the merit field, for example, there are many Buddhas—is so precious to us. Simply seeing it purifies our mind and plants the seed of liberation and enlightenment. And it is the same with circumambulating, prostrating or making offerings to it. We can cultivate merit, the cause to achieve realizations, liberation and enlightenment, in the field of merit twenty-four hours a day. The only problem is if from our side we don't bother to do it. Otherwise, there is no limitation from the side of the holy object. The merit field is not limited by season. It is not that you can only create merit by making offerings, circumambulating or prostrating in the morning, but not in the afternoon or at night. There is no question of being limited by time or season.

Of the five paths to enlightenment, the first is the path of merit, which has three levels: small, middling and great. When you achieve the great path of merit, you see numberless buddhas in Nirmanakaya aspect. At that time, when your mind is at that level, what you now see as statues you see as actual living buddhas. Later, when you become an arya being, you see buddhas in Sambhogakaya aspect. And when your mind is totally free from even subtle defilements, you actually see the Buddha mentally. You see yourself and the Buddha as one, with no separation. This is also the same when you achieve the guru. The absolute guru—the holy mind of all the buddhas, the transcendental wisdom of non-dual bliss and voidness—manifests to us through this ordinary aspect, which shows faults, delusions and suffering. This ordinary aspect, which fits our mistaken impure mind, is the only one that can guide us from happiness to happiness to enlightenment.

As I often advertise, we should have as many buddhas as possible in our house. But we should not put them on the floor or use them for decoration. We should respect the Buddha images and keep them out of devotion, by seeing the benefits that I have explained. We should have as many Buddhas as possible inside the house, and even outside, but placed respectfully. In this way anyone who comes into the house will be purified and without the need of words. Just by having holy objects such as stupas and statues around your house, you can liberate sentient beings from the lower realms every day by purifying their negative karma. In silence, without your needing to explain anything, the mere existence of the holy objects will liberate and bring to enlightenment the sentient beings—even flies or worms—who see, touch or circumambulate them. Without words you liberate these sentient beings. You bought, sponsored the making of, or built these holy objects, and every day the holy objects liberate sentient beings and bring them to enlightenment.

Offering light increases your Dharma wisdom and brings you the five types of clairvoyance. It also helps to prolong your life. And offering light to other sentient beings or illuminating an altar where there are holy objects instead of leaving it in darkness creates the karma, while you are in samsara, to never be born in a dark age, when no Buddha has descended and there are no teachings in the world. You are born only in an age of light, when a Buddha has descended and the Dharma exists in the world. You are born where Dharma exists and you then meet the Dharma.

Offering incense has many general benefits, as I mentioned before, but has the particular benefit of causing you to achieve a beautiful body. Also, even while you are in samsara, you will enjoy scented smells all the time. And you will be able to live in pure morality. The general benefits are the same for each offering, and then each offering has its particular benefits.

By offering flowers, you become a leader of others, like His Holiness the Dalai Lama and other holy beings, who receive the highest respect from other sentient beings. In that way you are then able to benefit others more. Because others respect you, they listen to you and follow you. If you give teachings they will listen to and then follow what you say. That is how you bring them from happiness to happiness to enlightenment. Also, the result of offering flowers is that your conduct becomes pure.

Offering medicine during the practice, as I mentioned the other day, helps you not to experience sickness while you are in samsara.

By offering food—the grains, for example—while you are in samsara, you don't experience famine. You are always able to find food, and the food is plentiful and healthy. You can always receive and enjoy crops, fruit, honey, milk and so forth. And the food you eat makes you healthy instead of harming your body.

By offering divine dress to the merit field, you are able to live in pure morality. It also causes you to receive a vajra holy body. Offering divine dress to Compassion Buddha causes you to achieve the vajra holy body of Compassion Buddha.

By offering ornaments, you create the karma to have great enjoyments, and you achieve the holy signs and exemplifications of the holy body of a Buddha.

Offering a vase purifies your negative karmas and delusions and helps you to generate loving kindness, compassion and bodhicitta in your heart.

Benefits of Circumambulations and Prostrations

Even doing one circumambulation of holy objects purifies past negative karmas, and because your past negative karmas are purified, you have no external enemies. Enemies are caused by past negative karma, so by purifying your past negative karma, you don't have any enemies. The ultimate benefit is that you purify completely even your subtle temporary defilements, or stains, and thus achieve the peerless happiness of enlightenment. Even one circumambulation directs your life toward that.

As you know, when you do prostrations, with each atom that is covered by your body, you create the merit to be born as a wheel-turning king one thousand times. No other king can be compared to a wheel-turning king, who is the most powerful king. A wheel-turning king controls one, two, three or four continents, and even the deva realms. To be born a wheel-turning king even one time you need to collect inconceivable merit. This is why, in the *Lankavatara Sutra*, Buddha used the example of a wheel-turning king to explain how much merit we collect when we do prostrations. When we lie down on the ground to do a prostration, which each atom that our body covers we collect the merit to be born as a wheel-turning king for one thousand lifetimes.

Now, when we do prostrations, even the small amount of finger-nail that projects from our fingers and the hair that covers the ground around us when we lie down covers an unimaginable number of atoms from here down to the bottom of the earth. This is without talking about the number of atoms covered by the rest of our body. It is like this with short hair, so imagine how many atoms our hair would cover if it were very long, if we had many feet of hair to cover the ground. If even our hair covers an unimaginable number of atoms when we do prostrations, there is no need to doubt about the rest of our body.

Therefore, in the Lama Tsong Khapa tradition, prostrations are much practiced, especially by the lineage lamas of the lam-rim. Even when Lama Atisha was very old and shaky, he still did many pros-trations every day. There are many stories in the Gelug tradition of lineage lamas of the lam-rim doing hundreds or even thousands of prostrations every day, especially with recitation of the names of the Thirty-five Buddhas. You can see now how doing prostrations is important, how it makes it easy to achieve all the realizations and enlightenment.

Also, by making offerings to or circumambulating Thousand-armed Chenrezig, we collect far greater merit than with other buddhas. This is a particular quality of Compassion Buddha, a result of his having dedicated in this way during the time he was a bodhisattva.

BENEFITS OF VOWS AND CHENREZIG PRACTICE

Also, merit increases unbelievably if one is living in the Eight Mahayana Precepts. This refers mainly to lay people, as novice monks and nuns have thirty-six vows and gelongs have many more—253 vows. For lay people who take the Eight Mahayana Precepts then do all these practices, the merit increases by an unbelievable factor and becomes very powerful.

There are four powers that enable one to collect extensive merit, the cause of happiness; this one is the power that comes from living in vows. As I often mention, if all the sentient beings in the three galaxies—or it could be the three realms (desire, form and formless realm)—became wheel-turning kings, and each one then made a light offering to Buddha using an ocean of butter with a wick the size of Mount Meru, all that merit could not equal that collected by one person living in ordination making a light offering to Buddha with butter the size of a mustard seed and a wick the size of a hair. The person living in ordination who made a tiny offering would collect far greater merit than all those other beings. So, if you are a layperson, if you take the Eight Mahayana Precepts then do all these practices, your merit increases by an unbelievable amount. That is a very skillful way to practice Dharma, enabling you to quickly achieve enlightenment.

Therefore, with stable devotion to Compassion Buddha, one-pointedly pray, then abide with your body, speech and mind in nyung-nä, or the retreat, reciting, offering mandalas, doing prostrations, circumambulating and making offerings. It says here that this brings the greatest profit in life. Therefore, put all your effort, all the energy you have, into this.

One very high Amdo lama, Kungthang Jampel Yang said, "If you are able to pray from your heart, doing a nyung-nä for just one day and reciting the six-syllable mantra can completely purify even the uninterrupted heavy karmas. These karmas definitely make you burn in the fire of the hells—and for how many lifetimes? For lifetimes equal to the number of atoms of this huge earth." Kungthang Jampel Yang was the founder of Tashi Khyil, the largest monastery in Amdo (not to be confused with Kumbum, the monastery on the site where Lama Tsong Khapa was born).

Tantric texts say that we have collected negative karma during beginningless rebirths, and that even in this life we have transgressed the three vows (pratimoksha, bodhisattva and tantric), collected much heavy negative karma in relation to the guru, to vajra brothers and sisters (which means those who have received initiation from the same guru), and to Buddha, Dharma and Sangha. And we have unconsciously enjoyed polluted food, which means food offered by other people out of devotion that we have eaten while not living purely in our vows. This polluted food is dangerous because it obscures our mind. It is regarded as a great obstacle to the achievement of realizations. Unconsciously eating polluted food and such things cause us to be born in the hell realms, specifically in the Hot and Great Hot hells. Kungthang Jampel Yang advises that people who have created such karmas have no other means but to put every single effort into this practice. He talks in this way about the power of the practice of the meditation-recitation of Compassion Buddha and the nyung-nä.

I will now give the oral transmission of the longest mantra of Compassion Buddha. In some of the Tibetan texts you may find some of the syllables are a little different, not only in this mantra, but in others.

[Rinpoche gives the oral transmission of the longest Chenrezig mantra, the long *dharani*, and OM MANI PADME HUM.]

I think that must be enough for this time.

I enjoyed the sessions that I attended here *very* much. I think this practice is really fantastic. It is something that you find more and more inspiring—not something that becomes more and more boring. The more sessions you do, the more inspiring it becomes. That is very good. The more you develop your compassion, the more you see the kindness of sentient beings and how much they are suffering, and you then don't find any hardship in doing retreat or nyungnä. Not finding any difficulty in doing the practice is a sign of receiving the blessing of the deity.

To end this, I would like to make just a small contribution of $US3,000 to the retreat; it's a small donation for food for the retreat people. And here I would like to thank again the benefactors and sponsors of this retreat. [Rinpoche reads out, with some entertaining pronunciations, the names of the benefactors and sponsors.]

Again here I would like to thank very much everyone who has been doing the retreat, especially the Sangha, who have been the main ones. From the bottom of my heart I thank all of you who have participated in any of the sessions from time to time. Thank you very, very much. And I thank very much also the sponsors and benefactors. It's always in my prayers, and I will dedicate the merits.

I think that is all. As the dedication we can recite *The King of Prayers*. We can include the people mentioned who have recently died, who are dying right now, or who are very sick. With this prayer, dedicate the merits we have collected during the three times, and especially today, for them to recover from their sicknesses.

This is a photo of the statue of Thousand-armed Chenrezig, which is about the same size, or maybe a little bigger, than the statue here. Denise Griffin, the artist who made the prototype for the large 500-foot Maitreya Buddha statue, made it. I asked her to make this Chenrezig statue for a nunnery at Pu Li in Taiwan. It's a nice small nunnery with two nuns—one is the abbess and the other is her student. I suggested to Denise that she make a Thousand-armed Compassion Buddha statue, so she made it there in Taiwan. The art of this Thousand-armed Chenrezig is the best that I have so far seen. You can see from the picture that it is very beautiful, except for the narrow base, which is a little sharp. The mantra at the top was written by His Holiness the Dalai Lama, who has signed it there. This is very good writing. I had this small picture made so that it could be put on an altar in a car. Normally I give people this card for their car. I don't give it for an altar in their bathroom, but they can put it on an altar in their car for protection, to remind them of bodhicitta, and many other reasons.

Maybe the Sangha can come first then the lay people. I'm not sure there will be enough cards—I hope there are enough to give one to everyone. And for the Sangha there is a very short zen, so short that it almost disappears....

Appendix 1

PRAYER FOR SPONTANEOUS BLISS

Respectfully I prostrate to the mighty protector, Maitreya,
Who pervades the world with clouds of love and compassion
From the space of Dharmakaya, which spontaneously completes great bliss,
And who rains down deeds in a continuous shower.

From your wisdom manifestation that sees, just as they are,
The minds and natural elements of countless disciples,
By the power of faith, please come down here in all places unimpeded,
Like the reflected image of the moon in water.

Like jeweled inlay work of many kinds of precious gemstones
Set into a Mt. Sumeru of piled exquisite refined gold,
Your supreme form, which when seen leaves one unsatisfied,
I request to remain firmly for as long as cyclic existence lasts.

You, protector, hold closely with your compassionate hands
All sentient beings who have provided the requirements
For constructing a statue of affectionate love [Maitreya], and
Please lead them definitely to the land of Tushita.

Inseparable from your face, amrita for their eyes,
Nurtured by your speech, the Mahayana scriptures,
And having perfected all the bodhisattva's practices,
Please bestow your blessings for them to quickly attain buddhahood.

In the meantime, may all wishes be fulfilled;
May all sentient beings have a loving attitude;
May the teachings of the Buddha spread and extend in all directions;
And may all sentient beings enjoy wonderful well being.

May this place be filled by an assembly of ordained monks and nuns
Clad in saffron robes and upholding the three trainings, and
May deeds of explanation and practice bring good fortune of extending
The Buddha's teachings everywhere for as long as cyclic existence lasts.

By the truth of the infallible three precious jewels,
The blessings of the power of Buddha Maitreya,
And the enlightened deeds of the mighty Dharma protectors,
May the complete essence of this pure prayer be fulfilled.

Colophon:

This aspiration prayer of truthful words for achieving excellence was composed at Chökhor Gyäl Monastery by His Holiness Gendun Gyatso [the Second Dalai Lama], a monk who expounds the Dharma, at the request of the great woman leader, Nyima Päl, an incarnation of Bishwakarma [the legendary King of Artistry who designed the main temple in central Lhasa]. Translated by Geshe Lhundup Sopa for members of the Maitreya Project, Singapore, February 1998. Revised edition, FPMT Education Department, June 1999.

Appendix 2

CHENREZIG FOOD OFFERING

First generate the motivation: "The purpose of my life is to free all sentient beings from all their suffering and its causes and bring them to full enlightenment; therefore, I must achieve enlightenment; therefore, I'm going to practice the yoga of eating, making food offering to the guru, Buddha, Dharma and Sangha and making charity to all sentient beings."

All the food in the kitchen is purified in emptiness. While it is empty, your wisdom understanding emptiness manifests in the syllable BHRUM, which transforms into an extensive jeweled container, inside of which is an OM. The OM, which symbolizes Buddha's holy body, speech and mind, melts into light and transforms into numberless oceans of uncontaminated nectar.

OM AH HUM (3x)

Offer numberless oceans of uncontaminated nectar to His Holiness the Dalai Lama, Compassion Buddha in human form, as well as to all the direct and indirect gurus, buddhas, bodhisattvas, arhats, dakas and dakinis, and Dharma protectors. The essence of all of them is your root virtuous friend. The nectar generates infinite bliss within them. Prostrate to all of them with your two palms together.

Offer numberless oceans of uncontaminated nectar to all the Buddhas, Dharma and Sangha of the ten directions, imagining that their essence is your root virtuous friend. They generate infinite bliss within them. Prostrate to all of them.

Offer numberless oceans of uncontaminated nectar to all the statues, stupas, scriptures and thangkas in all the universes of the ten directions, imagining that their essence is your root virtuous friend. They generate infinite bliss within them. Prostrate to all of them.

Make charity of numberless oceans of uncontaminated nectar to every hell being, every hungry ghost, every animal, every human being, every asura being, every sura being, every intermediate state being. They all fully enjoy the nectar and are liberated from all their suffering as well as its causes. They all become enlightened in the aspect of Compassion Buddha.

We have collected limitless skies of merit with our motivation of bodhicitta. We have collected limitless skies of merit by having made offering to Compassion Buddha and the rest of the merit field. We have collected limitless skies of merit by having made offering to all the Buddhas, Dharma and Sangha of the ten directions. We have collected four times limitless skies of merit by having made offering to all the statues, stupas, scriptures and thangkas of the ten directions. We have collected seven times limitless skies of merit by having made charity to all sentient beings. We have also collected so many times limitless skies of merit by having prostrated with our two palms together to Buddha, Dharma and Sangha and all the numberless holy objects.

la ma sang gyä la ma chö
de zhin la ma ge dün te
kün gyi je po la ma te
la ma nam la chö par bül

Due to all these merits, and the past and future merits collected by me and all the merits of the three times collected by others, may I, the members of my family, all the students and benefactors of the FPMT, and all other sentient beings never be separated from the guru-Triple Gem, always collect merit by making offerings, and receive the blessings of the guru-Triple Gem, which are all the realizations from guru devotion up to enlightenment, especially bodhicitta and clear light. May all these realizations be actualized within my own mind and in the minds of all sentient beings without even a second's delay.

Due to all the past, present and future merits collected by me and the merits of the three times collected by others (which are empty), may the I (which is empty) achieve enlightenment (which is empty) and lead all sentient beings (who are empty) to that enlightenment (which is empty) by myself alone (who is also empty).

Appendix 3

MANI RETREAT SCHEDULE

4:15 to 4:45	Eight Mahayana Precepts
5:00 to 6:30	*Combined Jorchö and Lama Chöpa Puja*
8:00 to 9:30	First mani session
10:00 to 11:30	Second mani session
3:30 to 5:00	Third mani session
6:00 to 8:00	Fourth mani session

NOTES

1 These are karmas so heavy that they ripen immediately as a rebirth in the hell realm upon the exhaustion of the karma of this life. The five are: killing one's mother, killing one's father, drawing the blood of a Buddha, killing an arhat and causing disunity among the Sangha.

2 The five close uninterrupted negative karmas are similar to the five uninterrupted negative karmas but slightly less grave. Nevertheless, they also result in rebirth in the hell realm upon the exhaustion of the karma of this life. These five are: killing a bodhisattva dwelling in certainty (i.e., one certain to achieve enlightenment within one hundred eons); killing an *arya*; destroying a stupa, monastery, temple etc. with hatred; raping a fully-ordained nun who is an arhat; appropriating the property of the Sangha.

3 Page numbers refer to *Nyung Nä: The Means of Achievement of the Eleven-Faced Great Compassionate One, Avalokiteshvara of the (Bhikshuni) Lakshmi Tradition*, composed by Losang Kälsang Gyatso, the Seventh Dalai Lama, compiled and translated by Lama Thubten Zopa Rinpoche and George Churinoff. Wisdom Publications: Boston, 1995.

THE ARCHIVE TRUST

The work of the Lama Yeshe Wisdom Archive falls into two categories: archiving and dissemination.

ARCHIVING requires managing the audiotapes of teachings by Lama Yeshe and Lama Zopa Rinpoche that have already been collected, collecting tapes of teachings given but not yet sent to the ARCHIVE, and collecting tapes of Lama Zopa's on-going teachings, talks, advice and so forth as he travels the world for the benefit of all. Tapes are then catalogued and stored safely while being kept accessible for further work.

We organize the transcription of tapes, add the transcripts to the already existent database of teachings, manage this database, have transcripts checked, and make transcripts available to editors or others doing research on or practicing these teachings.

Other archiving activities include working with videotapes and photographs of the Lamas and digitizing ARCHIVE materials.

DISSEMINATION involves making the Lamas' teachings available directly or indirectly through various avenues such as books for free distribution, regular books for the trade, lightly edited transcripts, audio- and videotapes, and articles in *Mandala* and other magazines, and on our Web site. Irrespective of the method we choose, the teachings require a significant amount of work to prepare them for distribution.

This is just a summary of what we do. The ARCHIVE was established with virtually no seed funding and has developed solely through the kindness of many people, some of whom we have mentioned at the front of this book.

Our further development similarly depends upon the generosity of those who see the benefit and necessity of this work, and we would be extremely grateful for your help.

THE ARCHIVE TRUST has been established to fund the above activities and we hereby appeal to you for your kind support. If you would like to make a contribution to help us with any of the above tasks or to sponsor books for free distribution, please contact us by any of the means shown above.

THE FOUNDATION FOR THE PRESERVATION OF THE MAHAYANA TRADITION

The Foundation for the Preservation of the Mahayana Tradition (FPMT) is an international organization of Buddhist meditation study and retreat centers, both urban and rural, monasteries, publishing houses, healing centers and other related activities founded in 1975 by Lama Thubten Yeshe and Lama Thubten Zopa Rinpoche. At present, there are more than 150 FPMT activities in twenty-eight countries worldwide.

The FPMT has been established to facilitate the study and practice of Mahayana Buddhism in general and the Tibetan Gelug tradition, founded in the fifteenth century by the great scholar, yogi and saint, Lama Je Tsong Khapa, in particular.

Every three months, the Foundation publishes a magazine, *Mandala,* from its International Office in the United States of America. To subscribe or view back issues, please go to the *Mandala* Web site, www.mandalamagazine.org, or contact:

FPMT
125B La Posta Rd., Taos, NM 87571, USA
Telephone (505) 758-7766; fax (505) 758-7765
fpmtinfo@fpmt.org
www.fpmt.org

Our Web site also offers teachings by His Holiness the Dalai Lama, Lama Yeshe, Lama Zopa Rinpoche and many other highly respected teachers in the tradition, details about the FPMT's educational programs, a complete listing of FPMT centers all over the world and in your area, and links to FPMT centers on the Web, where you will find details of their programs, and other interesting Buddhist and Tibetan home pages.

OTHER TEACHINGS OF
LAMA YESHE AND LAMA ZOPA RINPOCHE

BOOKS PUBLISHED BY WISDOM PUBLICATIONS

Wisdom Energy, by Lama Yeshe and Lama Zopa Rinpoche
Introduction to Tantra, by Lama Yeshe
Transforming Problems, by Lama Zopa Rinpoche
The Door to Satisfaction, by Lama Zopa Rinpoche
The Tantric Path of Purification, by Lama Yeshe
The Bliss of Inner Fire, by Lama Yeshe
Ultimate Healing, by Lama Zopa Rinpoche

A number of transcripts by Lama Yeshe and Lama Zopa Rinpoche are also available. For more information about these transcripts or the books mentioned above, see the Wisdom Publications Web site (www.wisdompubs.org) or contact Wisdom directly at 199 Elm Street, Somerville, MA 02144, USA, or Wisdom distributors such as Snow Lion Publications (USA), Wisdom Books (England) or Mandala Books (Australia).

VIDEOS OF LAMA YESHE

Available in either PAL or NTSC formats.

Introduction to Tantra: 2 tapes, US$40
The Three Principal Aspects of the Path: 2 tapes, US$40
Offering Tsok to Heruka Vajrasattva: 3 tapes, US$50

Shipping and handling extra. Available from LYWA, Mandala Books, Wisdom Books or Meridian Trust (London). Contact LYWA for more details or see our Web site, www.LamaYeshe.com.

What to do with Dharma teachings

THE BUDDHADHARMA IS THE TRUE SOURCE OF HAPPINESS for all sentient beings. Books like the one in your hand show you how to put the teachings into practice and integrate them into your life, whereby you get the happiness you seek. Therefore, anything containing Dharma teachings or the names of your teachers is more precious than other material objects and should be treated with respect. To avoid creating the karma of not meeting the Dharma again in future lives, please do not put books (or other holy objects) on the floor or underneath other stuff, step over or sit upon them, or use them for mundane purposes such as propping up wobbly tables. They should be kept in a clean, high place, separate from worldly writings, and wrapped in cloth when being carried around. These are but a few considerations.

Should you need to get rid of Dharma materials, they should not be thrown in the rubbish but burned in a special way. Briefly: do not incinerate such materials with other trash, but alone, and as they burn, recite the mantra OM AH HUM. As the smoke rises, visualize that it pervades all of space, carrying the essence of the Dharma to all sentient beings in the six samsaric realms, purifying their minds, alleviating their suffering, and bringing them all happiness, up to and including enlightenment. Some people might find this practice a bit unusual, but it is given according to tradition. Thank you very much.

Dedication

THROUGH THE MERIT CREATED by preparing, reading, thinking about and sharing this book with others, may all teachers of the Dharma live long and healthy lives, may the Dharma spread throughout the infinite reaches of space, and may all sentient beings quickly attain enlightenment.

In whichever realm, country, area or place this book may be, may there be no war, drought, famine, disease, injury, disharmony or unhappiness, may there be only great prosperity, may everything needed be easily obtained, and may all be guided by only perfectly qualified Dharma teachers, enjoy the happiness of Dharma, have love and compassion for all sentient beings, and only benefit and never harm each other.

LAMA THUBTEN ZOPA RINPOCHE was born in Thami, Nepal, in 1946. At the age of three he was recognized as the reincarnation of the Lawudo Lama, who had lived nearby at Lawudo, within sight of Rinpoche's Thami home. Rinpoche's own description of his early years may be found in his book, *The Door to Satisfaction* (Wisdom Publications). At the age of ten, Rinpoche went to Tibet and studied and meditated at Domo Geshe Rinpoche's monastery near Pagri, until the Chinese occupation of Tibet in 1959 forced him to forsake Tibet for the safety of Bhutan. Rinpoche then went to the Tibetan refugee camp at Buxa Duar, West Bengal, India, where he met Lama Yeshe, who became his closest teacher. The Lamas went to Nepal in 1967, and over the next few years built Kopan and Lawudo Monasteries. In 1971 Lama Zopa Rinpoche gave the first of his famous annual lamrim retreat courses, which continue at Kopan to this day. In 1974, with Lama Yeshe, Rinpoche began traveling the world to teach and establish centers of Dharma. When Lama Yeshe passed away in 1984, Rinpoche took over as spiritual head of the FPMT, which has continued to flourish under his peerless leadership. More details of Rinpoche's life and work may be found on the FPMT Web site, www.fpmt.org. Rinpoche's other published teachings include *Wisdom Energy* (with Lama Yeshe), *Transforming Problems, Door to Satisfaction, Bliss of Inner Fire* and *Ultimate Healing* and a number of transcripts and practice booklets (available from Wisdom at www.wisdompubs.org).

AILSA CAMERON first met Buddhism at Tushita Retreat Centre in India in 1983 and has since been involved in various activities within the FPMT, primarily in relation to the archiving, transcribing and editing of the teachings of Lama Zopa Rinpoche and Lama Yeshe. With Ven. Robina Courtin, she edited *Transforming Problems* and *The Door to Satisfaction*, by Lama Zopa Rinpoche, and *The Bliss of Inner Fire*, by Lama Yeshe, and more recently edited Rinpoche's *Ultimate Healing*. After working originally in India and Nepal, she went to Hong Kong in 1989 to help organize the electronic version of the Lama Yeshe Wisdom Archive. Ordained as a nun by His Holiness the Dalai Lama in 1987, she has been a member of the Chenrezig Nuns' Community in Australia since 1990. She is currently a full time editor with the Lama Yeshe Wisdom Archive.